The Books That Made Us

The Books That Made Us

*Deconstructing the
Modern Christian Classics*

∗∗∗

Rebecca Bratten Weiss

ORBIS BOOKS
Maryknoll, New York 10545

Orbis Books, the publishing arm of the Maryknoll Fathers and Brothers, endeavors to publish works that enlighten the mind, nourish the spirit, and challenge the conscience. To learn more about Maryknoll and Orbis Books, please visit our website at www.orbisbooks.com.

Published by Orbis Books, Box 302, Maryknoll, NY 10545-0302.

Manufactured in the United States of America.
Manuscript editing and typesetting by Joan Weber Laflamme.

Library of Congress Cataloging-in-Publication Data

Names: Bratten Weiss, Rebecca, author.
Title: The books that made us : deconstructing the modern Christian classics / Rebecca Bratten Weiss.
Description: Maryknoll, NY : Orbis Books, [2025] | Includes bibliographical references. | Summary: "Deconstructing and re-engaging beloved yet problematic Christian literary classics"— Provided by publisher.
Identifiers: LCCN 2025012482 (print) | LCCN 2025012483 (ebook) | ISBN 9781626986428 (trade paperback) | ISBN 9798888660973 (epub)
Classification: LCC Art & Religion (print) | LCC Art & Religion (ebook)
LC record available at https://lccn.loc.gov/2025012482
LC ebook record available at https://lccn.loc.gov/2025012483

Contents

Part Three
Tactics for Reading

Part One

Our Problematic Christian Literary Landscape

1

The Books That Made Us—
and Marred Us

A season of fragmentation

Thanks partially to the 2016 presidential election, my ties with old communities were fraying. When Trump loomed on the scene, I was an adjunct, teaching philosophy and literature at a conservative university. My co-workers were mostly devout Republicans, but also intellectuals who had spent their lives immersed in the classics of Western civilization. I assumed they would draw a line at supporting a candidate who failed to exemplify traditional values. We all know how that went. Within months, multiple acquaintances went from mocking Trump to defending him. When the infamous Access Hollywood tape was released, and everyone heard Trump boasting about assaulting women, I assumed this would be it. But the day after the tapes came out, the professor with whom I'd first studied T. S. Eliot circulated a memo begging us to overlook Trump's regrettably vulgar style and vote for him anyway.

Still, I refused to lose hope in my fellow intellectuals. Surely a community dedicated to faith and the classics would put more weight in the reasoned, eloquent explanations of virtuous philosophers than in crass rhetoric and a disinterest in facts. Surely people who published papers on Aristotle, Aquinas, Dante, and Shakespeare, who were familiar with Plato's warnings about tyranny, and conversant with the Catholic Church's teachings on the preferential option for the most vulnerable, wouldn't sell out the common good for the sake of a few empty promises. And a few stalwarts did hold out, articulating their opposition to Trump using Catholic social teaching or Christian personalism.

Knowing many felt pressured to vote for the Republican candidate because of the abortion issue, I spent much of 2016 using my writing platform to argue that Trump was not a viable pro-life option. I thought my impassioned pleas would make a difference. And in a way, they did. People turned on me. Friends sent me angry messages. Co-workers harassed me about my feminism, or the texts I assigned in class. One professor sent me a series of increasingly bizarre messages expressing his shock that I would assign Vladimir Nabokov's *Lolita* to an upper-level world literature class. He thought it was a dirty book.

What that professor didn't know was that I assigned *Lolita* alongside Azar Nafisi's memoir *Reading Lolita in Tehran*.

In her memoir, Nafisi describes her experiences as a literature professor in Iran at the time of the Islamic revolution, how her culture went rapidly from progressive to fundamentalist, under an extremist, theocratic regime. When the government made it mandatory for women to veil, Nafisi refused, and was fired from the University of Tehran. Later, she and a group of young women students organized a secret reading group. One of the forbidden works they read was *Lolita.*

My students, all women, were inspired. They drew comparisons between Nafisi's experiences under fundamentalist Islam and their own experiences with fundamentalist Christianity, including at our university. They shared stories about priests shaming them in the confessional, professors commenting on their bodies or their clothing. Nafisi describes how in *Lolita,* the predator Humbert not only rapes Lolita and deprives her of her freedom, but he overwrites her story. My students talked about ways their own stories had been overwritten: by authoritarian fathers, patriarchal institutions, even the church.

In the summer of 2017, several faculty members went to the dean with a petition asking him to terminate my contract. The petition included accusations of things I hadn't done, including participating in the first Women's March (which I supported, but couldn't afford to attend). The dean acquiesced. I was out of a job.

At first I told only a few close friends about these circumstances, but after a conservative publication did an extensive hit piece about me, word of my termination got out. That was when I realized how isolated I was. A few people in my local community were supportive, but others, though happy to keep me in their social circles, made it clear that they had no intention of taking my side. Others appeared to find the whole thing amusing. I tried to take this stoically and think of it as part of our nation's general dystopian comedy.

The rise of a government leader making false claims, questioning democracy, and demonizing people on the margins was alarming. Being noisy and obnoxious about my concerns has, in one way, paid off. It helped me find a new community, an online circle of smart, empathetic, quirky people, mostly Christian, some of them artists and writers. In our virtual space, we pondered questions of identity, justice, and art, and raged about the state of our nation and church. Those communities sustained me through the chaotic years of the first Trump administration.

Everything became strange and uncertain when the COVID-19 pandemic began. Then, on Easter Sunday 2020, my father died of heart failure, and it felt like a whole world had crumbled.

Not because I depended on my father—he never held a job in all the years I knew him, never had a bank account, never paid taxes. My family was even homeless for a time, after we were kicked out of the Protestant community where we'd lived for nine years. My sister and I were in college at the time. For a while, my parents and our little brother stayed with one of Dad's strange friends, in a low-income neighborhood downtown. Dad hated it there, not because it was low income, but because it was city. He wanted to be out in the country, gardening and planting orchards. One evening, fed up, he stole a bottle of vodka from a convenience store and drank it in his truck while listening to the news on the radio. Mom called me at the house where I worked as a nanny to tell me he was in jail. Since she had no money, my sister and I pooled our babysitting cash to bail out our father. So no, we didn't depend on him, but the idea of a world without him made no sense. He was too vast a presence to just vanish.

Dad went to his grave leaving little of material worth, but a treasure trove of stories that my family heard many times but never got all the details on. There was the story about learning Esperanto so he could start a political party in Brazil. The story about being hired to work for Robert F. Kennedy: "His people liked my ideas. They gave me a desk." There was the story about being kicked out of the Coast Guard and locked up for being a conscientious objector. This one never quite lined up for us. Eventually we figured out that he'd been incarcerated in the infamous NARCO farm in Lexington, Kentucky, where blues musicians went to detox, and Thomas Merton occasionally hung out, and the CIA carried out some of its notorious MKUltra mind-control experiments. Was the CIA responsible for the wacky life we'd lived? My siblings and I could theorize for hours, but any answers Dad had he took to his grave.

My sense of self was fragmenting. My job was gone. My father was gone. People I'd trusted had become unrecognizable. I mulled over questions like "what do I even believe anymore?" Or "why have I put up with people who treated me badly?" I began to pay attention to the discrepancy between gospel values and the things that went on in Christian spaces. Why had my fellow Catholics capitulated so quickly to Trump? Why did my supposed friends not stand up for me?

As people across the nation died and mourned and bodies were put into freezer trucks because the morgues were full, I mourned the loss of my father. I knew I would never know the full details of his story, but maybe I could get a better grasp of my own.

Recruited for the culture war

As part of my project of trying to understand who I was, where I had come from, and where I belonged, I dug into my old journals from teenage years. I expected to be mortified by my teenage self—and I was. But I also found her likable. The person archived in those pages was ridiculous but also funny and perceptive, someone my kids might have been friends with. I read about my years working at a Christian ranch, my crushes, my outrage at hypocritical and coercive religious authorities. My teenage rebellions (swigging beer on trail rides, kissing boys by the lake) looked silly, compared with later, more extravagant rebellions. But my excitement when I had the chance to talk to other bookish nerds felt familiar. So did my enthusiasm to be off to college.

But shortly after the start of my freshman year, the tone of the journals changed. My empathy dwindled, my judgments grew incoherent, and my prose became embarrassingly ornate, as though I was attempting, and failing, to emulate a Victorian essayist. There was a lot of navel-gazing under the guise of spirituality. The worst was reading about my trip to DC for the March for Life. Did I really write those derogatory judgments about pro-choice feminists? The thoughtful, quirky teenager was gone, replaced by an unpleasant foot soldier for the religious right. I had to ask: What happened?

It had nothing to do with rejecting education. I was an ambitious student, double majoring in philosophy and literature, and enrolled in a four-year Great Books seminar. In my spare time, I sat under trees reading Aristotle and Aquinas, underlining furiously. In the company of the intellectual greats of Christendom, I should have flourished. That's the promise of a humanities education, right? That good books make good people.

One of my favorite quotations about reading is from George R. R. Martin's *A Dance with Dragons*: "A reader lives a thousand lives before he dies." But love of books doesn't always correlate with virtue. Thomas Jefferson, a voracious reader of the classics, kept Sally Hemings in a position of sexual slavery for forty years. The great modernist poet Ezra Pound, steeped in the classics of Christendom, was an antisemite who admired Mussolini. And Heidegger, widely regarded as one of the most significant philosophers of the twentieth century, was a Nazi. Loving good books is not enough to make a good person.

MY GREAT BOOKS PROGRAM started with the Homeric epics and ended with the moderns. Between the ancient world and the Victorian era, the reading list hardly varied from one class section to the next, but the twentieth century posed a conundrum. Suddenly teachers couldn't agree on which writers were important. Some assigned their niche favorites, maybe a French novelist or Austrian economist, names we'd barely heard of. The important thing was that they were Catholic, or at least Christian, or at least conservative. Our teachers ignored most of the significant writers of the twentieth century in favor of lesser-known writers who were a better fit for the university's ultra-conservative ideology. No longer were we exploring the world through books; we were retreating to a fortress, armed with our preferred texts.

The dilemma was clear. We were supposed to be reading books that would form our hearts and minds according to a certain mold. For centuries, "the classics of Western civilization" implied a Christian milieu, but in the modern era this was no longer the case, so could these books really be considered formative, or even safe? It was easy enough, in earlier centuries, to assign a bunch of Christian writers, then throw in a token dissenter like Rousseau or Nietzsche. But few of the landmark texts of the twentieth century, even those by white male Europeans, can be shoehorned into a culture-war agenda. As conservative Christians we'd staked a claim to the

Western tradition, but it had gotten away from us. Literature and philosophy were now dominated by feminists, Marxists, deconstructionists, queer theorists, and post-colonial writers who critiqued Christianity's alliance with imperialism. Definitely not on our team.

Meanwhile, the world of Christian letters became more self-conscious of its status as Christian. And an unofficial canon of Great Modern Christian Literature emerged. All the criticisms of the broader literary canon (it's insufficiently diverse, it's self-subverting, it's a social construct) are true of this sub-canon. But like many social constructs, it sticks around. Sign up for a class on Christianity and Literature, or go to a conference on the Christian Imagination, and you will encounter the same names: G. K. Chesterton. C. S. Lewis. Evelyn Waugh. J. R. R. Tolkien. Flannery O'Connor. It would hardly be a Christian literary event without them.

As a youthful culture warrior eager to articulate an intellectually robust identity, this literary tradition was just what I was looking for. I could set myself above both the evangelicals who had shamed me for my rebellion, and the well-off secular kids who had bullied me for being a weirdo. I could make Christian culture my own, and perform it in my own way, which didn't have to be boring or lowbrow. I'd found my witty, sophisticated "in group," who were dead and couldn't police me. All I had to do to fit in was read the right books and telegraph the right social codes, including quoting Latin poems, or enjoying good port (or not so good port, given my finances). It did not occur to me for many years why Latin poems and port should be part of a Christian ethic. It didn't matter, because I'd found my niche.

Looking back, I realize I'd tumbled into a toxic fan culture. We were wildly, uncharitably critical of everything outside that culture, but almost completely uncritical of ourselves or the writers we looked up to. Their ideas shaped my artistic tastes, even the clothes I wore (a pathetic attempt at Edwardian). I once read an essay by Hilaire Belloc (who I will not be discussing in the chapters ahead) in which he ranted about his hatred of the piano. This worried me. I loved the piano. Sometimes I met up in the piano lounge for a bizarre ongoing flirtation with a fellow amateur pianist. I didn't worry about the flirtation being unethical, but I did worry about the piano being vulgar. I should have said, "Sorry, Belloc, you're wrong," but we were primed to criticize everything except our intellectual heroes. So much for my avowals of objectivity.

Anyone who has lived in a conservative Christian subculture has probably experienced that pressure to make it your entire personality. Like a cult, there are no shades of gray. Anyone who isn't on your side is suspect. Any authority in the community must be admired. And everything has to support a specific conception of Christian morality.

MOST OF US RECOGNIZE that art relates to a culture's norms. Political propagandists and advertisers capitalize on stories and images that influence our moral sense. Arguments about book bans highlight our collective understanding that art is about more than entertainment. Even in the world of popular art, discussions are often more about morals than about aesthetics. At my school, there was the added dimension of religion. Our books were supposed to make us better Christians.

So, did it work? At the time I thought it did. But maybe this depends on what "Christian" means. Given the way white Christians rallied behind Trump in both 2016 and 2024, I can understand why people might associate Christianity with bigotry and general unpleasantness. By those standards, I was a great Christian.

The stories we tell ourselves

But those journal entries worry me. If I had continued on that path, how would I have responded to the first Trump campaign? I still think I would have been too much of a snob to support the MAGA movement.

But I did not stay on that trajectory. Shortly after grad school, following a series of unfortunate events and bad decisions, I had a breakdown of sorts, and set forth on a path of creative self-destruction. Somehow, throughout it all, I continued to go to Mass. I even continued to defend conservative values while violating them. During my brief first marriage, I argued vehemently against installing condom machines in the bathroom of the bar my ex owned, because they would "encourage people to make immoral choices."

Eventually, friends and family helped me get back on my feet. I was motivated, too, by the memory of a better time, when I was a goofy adolescent riding horses and declaiming poetry. I wanted to be that person again. There's a passage in Dostoevsky's *The Brothers Karamazov* about how a person can be saved by a single happy memory, and I had many. I began to rebuild my life.

So in 2016, I was teaching at the same university that had radicalized me to ultra-conservatism in my late teen years, but my mindset had changed. Finally, I was claiming my independence, questioning precepts, inching toward a more progressive value system. Given my workplace and social situation, this was not a convenient moral evolution, and I knew I was on thin ice at the university, so I made sure to back up my arguments with magisterial Catholic teaching, in hopes that a little diversity of opinion, within the bounds of orthodoxy, would be welcome. Most of my students welcomed it at least. During my time as a teacher, I had the privilege of teaching hundreds of smart, questioning young people, and they may have given me too optimistic a view of our subculture.

My surprise, when I learned I was wrong about my fellow intellectuals, came from a place of privilege. I realize this now. Being ethnically Jewish, I have experienced antisemitism. As a woman, I've experienced misogyny. I was bullied as a teenager because of my family's lifestyle. But I'm still a white straight person with decent health. And I'm not just an innocent bystander; in the past, I helped prop up movements of hate and exclusion. Since 2016, I've tried to be honest and hold myself accountable, but the story isn't just about me. It's about our history, language, metaphors. It's about the stories we tell ourselves, including the stories about who we are.

One story we Christians tell ourselves is that our religion has always been a force for good—that the church is the best ally women ever had, that it always opposed injustice, stood with the poor, fought racism. In some times and places, this has been true, but in others, we've been oppressors, colonizers, and warmongers. Even when we haven't directly enacted injustice, we've been sluggish about opposing it. The Catholic Church—the oldest and most powerful Christian denomination, which claims to teach with divine authority—didn't even condemn slavery until the twentieth century.[1] In movements for women's suffrage, many religious leaders didn't just stand on the sidelines; they actively opposed women's rights.

Today, white Western Christians wield significant influence in public life, have churches on every corner, have our emblems in public spaces, our rituals at public events, our major feasts as national holidays. Various Christian groups get special loopholes, and not always for commendable things: Christians can get away with denying their kids needed healthcare on the basis of their faith. Our legal system respects the Catholic seal of confession. And we've repeatedly used our privilege in the public square, not to enact the principles of the gospel—not to ensure that the hungry are fed and the homeless housed—but to oppose desegregation, or to attack healthcare initiatives. This is the stark reality of history. As scholar and activist Erna Kim Hackett observes:

---

[1] Jacob Kohlhaas, "When Did the Church Condemn Slavery?" *US Catholic*, November 6, 2023.

White Christianity suffers from a bad case of
Disney princess theology. As each individual reads
Scripture, they see themselves as the princess in
every story. They are Esther, never Xerxes or Ha-
man. They are Peter, but never Judas. They are
the woman anointing Jesus, never the Pharisees.
They are the Jews escaping slavery, never Egypt.
For citizens of the most powerful country in the
world, who enslaved both Native and Black people,
to see itself as Israel and not Egypt when studying
Scripture is a perfect example of Disney princess
theology.[2]

Disney princess theology means we are forever congratulating ourselves, and this seeps into our cultural discourse,
too, with ideas about Christian artists having a special relationship with truth and goodness, a unique capacity to draw
people to God. Such assumptions lie behind the readings lists
in Christian education. Among my co-religionists, the preferred term is *the Catholic imagination.* There's even a Catholic
imagination conference, which has been held annually since
poet Dana Gioia organized the first in 2015.

If the claims about Christian art are true, we should see
evidence. Gospel values should illuminate Christian literary
culture. I am not saying Christian artists and scholars should

---

[2] Erna Kim Hackett, "Why I Stopped Talking about Racial Reconciliation and Started Talking about White Supremacy," *Inheritance* (March
25, 2020).

all be saints, but we should see the difference faith makes, the courage to stand against injustice and bear witness to the Beatitudes. Our lives, even when messy and imperfect, should be visible signs of the invisible reality of divine grace. It's not enough to point to vague ideas or symbols. To take a line from Flannery O'Connor, "If it's just a symbol, to hell with it."

Part of our Disney princess theology involves thinking we Christians are always under attack. Our persecution complex spills over into our literary culture, too. Gioia, in his 2013 essay "The Catholic Writer Today," argues that "the cultural establishment views faithful Catholics with suspicion, disdain, or condescension."[3] I question this thesis. Catholic academics are employed all over the nation. Plenty of widely admired writers, both literary and popular, are Catholic, or Christians of a different denomination. Marilynne Robinson, David Lodge, Seamus Heaney, Donna Tartt, Toni Morrison, Mary Karr, Louise Erdrich, Jericho Brown, Alice McDermott, Mary McGarry Morris, Dean Koontz, Cormac McCarthy, Colm Toibín—it's a diverse list, but everyone on it is an extremely successful recent writer, and a Christian of some sort.

It's true, as Gioia says, that there's no "vital or influential" Catholic tradition in mainstream literary culture. This is even more an issue for other denominations. Is this the fault of the literary establishment, however? Or is it that secular literary spaces do more to foster real artistic engagement than

---

[3] Dana Gioia, "The Catholic Writer Today," *First Things,* December 2013.

religious ones do? We might not have the robust Christian literary society Chesterton, Sayers, Lewis, or O'Connor enjoyed, but our academic, literary, and entertainment worlds are full of Christians making overtly Christian-themed art. The Christian faith is not unwelcome among the educated class. As for the writers of the modern canon, people may criticize Eliot, Waugh, Lewis, Tolkien, O'Connor, and the rest, but they're all over reading lists, and influential in popular culture. The popularity of our art makes it all the more essential that we honestly assess its influence—on ourselves, on our literary culture, on the broader world.

2

Deconstructing the Imagination

What is deconstruction?

At some point, I started using the word *deconstruction* to describe my process of reevaluation. As an academic, I found the term apt. Soon, however, I learned others were using the term in a similar way, especially in evangelical spaces. I was part of a Zeitgeist. In the decade between 2010 and 2020, a number of influential evangelicals were publicly questioning long-held articles of faith. In 2016, writer and podcaster Blake Chastain coined the term *ex-vangelical* to describe his rejection of white evangelical Christianity. Writer Rachel Held Evans, scholar Pete Enns, and pastor Nadia Boltz-Weber led thoughtful conversations about faith, ethics, and the church's many failures to follow Jesus's teachings. Revelations about abuse or hypocrisy on the part of church leaders jump-started some of this questioning, but intellectual rigorousness was also a factor. People were tired of forcing themselves to assent to principles that didn't hold water. Suddenly the phrase *religious deconstruction* was everywhere.

Author Kristen Lavalley helpfully put together a time-line of religious deconstruction on her substack.[1] The concept of deconstruction, Lavalley notes, originated in the 1960s with philosopher Jacques Derrida. Today, if I were to send thank-you cards to dead philosophers, Derrida would be one of them, but I didn't appreciate his thought until after I had completed my master's degree in philosophy. In that program, I almost never heard his name, and when I did, it was usually with a note of warning. Derrida, along with Marx, Nietzsche, Freud, and a host of unruly feminists, was one of the bad guys, intent on demolishing objective truth, likely for sinister or hedonistic purposes.

Once I got over my brief stint as a culture warrior, I found this approach to the philosophical tradition—dividing thinkers into friends or foes—embarrassing. I was embarrassed by my whole academic scene. Excited as I'd been to escape the boondocks and head off to college, I hadn't found the enchanted door I was looking for. I was not at Oxford, eating strawberries and drinking rare wines à la *Brideshead Revisited*. For all my pretensions, I was in an intellectual backwater. Yet this backwater has, in the years since, grown and overflowed into the mainstream. The ultra-conservative, reactionary ideas that were standard at my university are now influencing national politics.

---

[1] Kristin Lavalley, "A Cultural History of Deconstruction." *Things I'm Thinking About*, September 5, 2023.

By the time I started my doctoral studies at another university, I had moved toward a more classically liberal position. My program was moderately conservative but more academically rigorous, the professors more invested in engaging with contemporary scholarship. Finally I had a chance to study different critical theories, and finally I read Derrida. He seemed like a trickster figure at first. But actually, he was offering me a path to humility and liberation—things I desperately needed.

It's not necessary to understand academic deconstructionism in order to understand religious deconstruction, but the two are connected. Deconstruction is fundamentally anti-institutional. It is suspicious of definitions, not because it rejects reality, but because it acknowledges that definitions can never fully reflect or contain reality. Deconstructionism looks at the assumptions latent in a system—for instance, assumptions about light versus dark, or white versus black, in our metaphors, and how these assumptions are present in other systems. It looks at the paradoxes in language by which a text can mean both one thing and its opposite—like the word "cleave," which can mean "join together" but also "split apart." To deconstruct a system of meaning is not to attack it, but to show how it functions.

Many of our edifices of meaning are human inventions, though we treat them as immutable essences. Take gender roles. They are real, but only because we invented them. Far from being fixed and immutable, they change from one culture to the next. But people want to treat them like eternal truths, and enforce them, sometimes violently. Deconstructionism looks at political motivations, too, which is one reason authoritarians find it threatening. It shouldn't be controversial to note that language is a construct, but you can see why this and other deconstructionist ideas might annoy religious dogmatists. Deconstructionism is not an attack on meaning as such, however. Nor is it incompatible with faith. Philosophers such as Jean-Luc Marion and John Caputo have applied its methods within a framework of religious belief.

Religious deconstruction is more informal and personal, though just as threatening to authoritarians. Deconstructors are suspicious of institutions that try to control religious realities. Rather than finding excuses for contradictions in religious rules, deconstructors look more closely at the ambiguities and assumptions latent in our edifices of meaning—like, if a person has to share Jesus's gender in order to be a priest, why not Jesus's ethnicity? Deconstruction often yields the conclusion that many of the sacred institutions implemented by churches are really human inventions. This doesn't mean deconstruction is incompatible with religious belief, however. There is no one path of deconstruction, and while many lead out of the church, others lead to a deeper, more authentic faith.

My relationship with the church? It's complicated

Among Catholics, a major impetus for deconstruction was the clergy sex-abuse crisis. That the church continued to insist on its own moral authority on sexual matters, while revelation after revelation unfolded, was unsupportable for many faithful churchgoers. They began to wonder what else the church might be wrong about, and noted things like how long it took for the Vatican to condemn slavery, or Pope Paul VI deciding not to reverse the ban on contraception, despite the advice of most of his advisers. The abuse crisis began to look like the latest in a long line of moral missteps.

A lot of this was happening in predominantly white spaces. Black, Indigenous, and other non-white believers were already aware of profound and systemic issues, and trying to hold their churches to gospel standards. Nevertheless, the 2016 presidential election accelerated a process that was already ongoing, especially for those who had suffered in their efforts to conform to conservative Christian rules. Many women had sacrificed their health to obey Catholic prohibitions on contraception. Queer Christians had hidden their identities. It was disorienting for those who, in their efforts to meet the standards of their faith communities, had endured personal loss or suffering, to see church leaders seeming not to take their own precepts seriously, after all. And this sudden jettisoning of long-held principles wasn't happening to accommodate the vulnerable, but to excuse the behavior of a powerful businessman known for his racist and misogynistic rhetoric, who had publicly mocked a handicapped person—a man who later would be charged for statutory assault and numerous financial crimes, and who would claim that he could murder and not be held accountable.

Some of the women in my social circles began to notice that abusive dynamics in their marriages mirrored those in their churches. Sometimes stepping away from a faith community led to further steps away from toxic and coercive relationships. In some cases, faith communities rallied to support abusers. Several writers, including Kaya Oakes, Angela Denker, and Sarah Stankorb, addressed the phenomenon of Christian groups protecting powerful abusers at the expense of their victims. I have seen it happen: the women walk away, while the men who abused them remain in their churches and communities.

The spectacle of Catholics embracing the MAGA movement pushed me over a line. I began to wonder why I had put up with authoritarian hypocrisy so long. Because I was ashamed of my own moral failings? Now I felt I could openly ask the questions I'd pondered for years: Is it a sin to be queer? Is birth control morally wrong? Are there only two genders? Are women supposed to be subordinate to men? Does God hate divorce?

I also began to look differently at some of the writers and thinkers I had long revered. When people shared quotes from G. K. Chesterton, C. S. Lewis, or Flannery O'Connor, with an air of invoking a higher authority, I found myself pushing back. I found myself saying things like, "Okay, but what if they were wrong?"

Deconstructors often point to institutional religion's failure to live up to Jesus's teachings. They may stick with Christianity despite the church, because of their love for Jesus. Or they might stay because they're attached to their communities, or because they want to work for reform. Some switch parishes or denominations. Some find new ways to live their faith, drawing on feminist, womanist, queer, and liberation theologies. Many who step away from their churches still identify as Christians—but others leave. The trend of religious deconstruction has contributed to the decline of Christianity. In Western Europe, once the cultural center of Christendom, a majority of the population identifies as nonpracticing Christian. In 1970, about 90 percent of people in the United States identified as Christians, according to a 2022 study.[2] In 2020 that percentage was down to 63 percent. Data from early 2025 indicated a leveling off, but it's worth noting that some of this is attributable to more men becoming Christian. Women, who for decades identified as more religious, are leaving their churches in record numbers.

If the 2020 rates of disaffiliation continue, fewer than 50 percent of people in the United States will identify as Christian by 2070.

In my culture-warrior days, we talked about people who left our faith as moral failures, hedonists resentful of morality. Traditional-leaning Christians still talk as though our culture were careening into anarchic depravity. "Why are people leaving?" our church leaders ask. And they conclude that we need more Bible study, more catechesis, a eucharistic congress, a

---

[2] "Modeling the Future of Religion in America," Pew Research Center, September 13, 2022.

devotional app. But the people who leave are far beyond that. Many are extremely well educated about Christian doctrine.

And deconstruction is rarely hedonistic. It is more likely to be wearying, unsettling, and lonely. Far from succumbing to peer pressure, deconstructors tend to be morally stubborn, willing to stand alone if they have to. Some lose friends, support systems, and social capital. Some leave marriages. They relinquish beliefs that were superficially comforting and aimed at quelling questions, like "it's all in God's hands" or "God never gives you more than you can handle," or "just pray about it." No, deconstruction is not for the weak.

Difficult though it is, it's a chance to start again.

The role of the imagination

Since I am a book nerd, my deconstruction process has involved analyzing my relationships with the thinkers who influenced my early formation. The "Christian imagination" people are right. The arts are not just about entertainment. They guide how we envision the world, and how we live our lives. So what happens if the literature we read depicts heroes exclusively as white, slender, and conventionally attractive? In which queer characters are always presented as sinister, labor activists as rabble rousers, Black characters as figures of ridicule—and in which massive societal injustices are simply ignored? Especially if this literature is well written, with sophisticated plots, complex characters, intelligent dialogue, engrossing themes, and striking figures of speech?

The modern Christian classics that formed me—and marred me—couldn't have had that effect unless they were beautifully crafted and at least partially aligned with reality. From an aesthetic standpoint, these are mostly good books, and some are even great books. We treat these writers as the gold standard for Christian creatives today, including when we fret over there not being enough good Christian writers anymore. ("Where is the next Evelyn Waugh? Where is the next Flannery O'Connor?") Part of the reason we have this anxiety about our literature is that we view it as a vehicle for evangelization. If the broader secular culture doesn't take our literature seriously, it's harder for us to convert people.

When I selected Christian writers to revisit as part of my practice of deconstruction, I had two main requirements. They needed to be taken seriously by a wider audience, and they needed to be practicing Christians, as opposed to people brought up as Christians who left the church. They did not have to be notably pious or holy, however. Looking over reading lists and conference subjects, and reflecting on my education, I settled on these nine writers: G. K. Chesterton, T. S. Eliot, Dorothy Sayers, Evelyn Waugh, Graham Greene, C. S. Lewis, J. R. R. Tolkien, Flannery O'Connor, and Walker Percy. Others could be added to the list, but these are the ones who formed my idea of what it meant to be a Christian writer.

Rereading their works, I tried to immerse myself in their imaginative worlds, while still staying alert and critical. Sometimes my reading prompted questions about the writers' lives or beliefs. Sometimes specific themes jumped out as important. But my overarching focus was on how these works affect the mind of a young reader. If my imagination was evangelized, what was it being evangelized into?

Part Two

Revisiting the Classics

3

G. K. Chesterton

Crunchy Chestertonians

My life was irrevocably shaped by the big dreams of my father. After his various adventures, Dad launched a career as a bar owner, met my mother, then dropped out of society with the intention of founding a Catholic agrarian community. Too stubborn and independent to join any community that already existed, he used to visit Dorothy Day at her Catholic Worker farm and argue with her about how they managed their gardens. He thought she should have made "her people" weed the cabbages more often.

Finally, in the 1990s, my parents found their people: a small group of Catholics involved with a startup magazine advancing agrarianism, personalism, and communitarianism. Though socially conservative on marriage, sex, and family life, the group distanced itself from the militarism, capitalism, and materialism associated with the Republican party. They were all about big families getting back to the land, practicing traditional arts. Their inspirations were medieval monastic life, Day's Catholic Worker movement, and the niche socioeconomic movement known as distributism, developed and popularized by Catholic writers G. K. Chesterton and Hilaire Belloc in the early twentieth century. Chesterton, especially, was our patron and hero. I was introduced to his writing as a teenager and, once I'd switched from rebel agnostic to obnoxious theist, tried to imitate his writing. Badly, of course.

In the early 2000s, conservative writer Rod Dreher coined the term *crunchy cons* to describe right-wingers who were getting back to the land. But my family was living it long before he described it. Looking back on those days, I remember artists and intellectuals gathered around bonfires, feasts of homegrown produce, people playing fiddles, and Irish dancing. It seemed so wholesome. Yet today, many of the people from that circle have swung far to the right. They believe the lies about immigrants. They mock LGBTQ people, and make jokes about wokeness. And they still love Chesterton, who, I think, would have despised Trump as a humorless, avaricious, capitalistic bully.

The man of many faces

Two Chestertons exist in my mind. One I associate with those cheery memories. The other I associate with creepy men who think Catholicism is all about smoking pipes, drinking heavily, and mocking minorities. And in my mind that second version has overshadowed the first. So when I decided to revisit Chesterton to launch this reading project, I was prepared to be annoyed.

I started with his 1908 thriller *The Man Who Was Thursday*. And to my surprise, I enjoyed it. There was the Chesterton who had enchanted me in my teens, by turns whimsical, melancholy, comical, outrageous, a person with a profound sense of both the tragic and the absurd.

That's "Good Chesterton." A man who was sympathetic to Bolsheviks, and critical of capitalism. Who made fun of bankers and businessmen. Who wrote poetically about donkeys, sunsets, romance, and cheese. Who understood the sickness unto death, the despair of modern life, the need to set out and wander, until you've gone around the world and, footsore and bedraggled, you crest the hill and you see your home again, with the lights shining, the most beautiful sight you can imagine.

But then there's "Bad Chesterton," who made snide comments about feminism, and opposed divorce, even in the case of physical abuse. He used racial slurs in his stories, and was both Islamophobic and antisemitic. He suggested that Jews should wear special identifying clothing and claimed there were "healthy elements in Hitlerism."

Who was he, really? Smug pipe-smoking crank, whimsical poet of donkeys and cheese, facile apologist for conservative Christianity, firebrand anti-capitalist—or all of these?

THESE DAYS, ONE ISN'T likely to encounter many conversations about Chesterton outside a very specific type of Catholic circle. But he was a tremendously recognizable figure in his time, known for his essays, novels, poems, and popular apologetics. Born into a middle-class family in Kensington, London, in 1874, Gilbert Keith Chesterton was baptized into the Church of England, though his family was Unitarian. His youthful interests included art and the occult, and he studied to be an illustrator at the Slade School, but he did not shine academically and left after three years, without taking a degree. In 1901 he married Frances Blogg, who drew him back to the Anglican Church. Later he converted to Catholicism. The Chestertons maintained a strong, affectionate relationship until Chesterton's death from heart failure in 1936. They never had children.

Chesterton started his career as a writer by working in publishing houses, while reading and writing extensively. He considered himself a journalist, but also wrote essays, poems, and stories. His nonfiction writing encompasses social and literary criticism, politics, theology, and apologetics. Ideas associated with Chesterton include the poetry of the ordinary, the primacy of common sense, the romance of the local, reverence for tradition, and a fascination with the uncanny, the sense that the world we live in is a repository of hidden meanings.

Originally a liberal, he shifted toward more conservative positions over time, especially once he converted to Catholicism. While Dale Ahlquist of the Chesterton Society has stated that there is little noticeable difference between his pre-conversion and post-conversion writing, I disagree. Earlier Chesterton, pre-conversion, is more whimsical and open to wonder, less aggressively certain, less smug, less deliberately bigoted. Yet from first to last Chesterton continued to defend the poor and the working class while critiquing the wealthy and privileged. And he held onto his sense of the enchantment in the ordinary.

The Man Who Was Thursday is one of his more popular fiction works, along with *The Napoleon of Notting Hill,* *The Flying Inn,* and the Father Brown detective stories. Though a popular public figure in his day, he was also taken seriously enough to be nominated for the Nobel Prize in Literature in 1935. Writers who have cited him as an influence include George Orwell, F. Scott Fitzgerald, Dorothy Sayers, Jorge Luis Borges, Agatha Christie, and Dean Koontz. He was good friends with Irish writer and socialist George Bernard Shaw, with whom he often debated. Others with whom he had friendly public debates included Bertrand Russell and H. G. Wells.

Chesterton was especially close with Catholic essayist, historian, and political activist Hilaire Belloc, with whom he collaborated in developing the socioeconomic system of distributism, a "third way" between capitalism and socialism. Distributism has been put into practice only in a few cases and on a micro level, but it remains a popular theory among some Catholics and is closely associated with Chesterton's legacy. Belloc was even more antisemitic than Chesterton, which may have been a factor in the latter's stubborn refusal to admit that his critics, on this score, had a point.

Not just a person of his time

Though I'd read some of his essays and detective stories earlier, my first sense of Chesterton as a person was through his collection *The Coloured Lands,* a compilation of lighthearted poems, sketches, and short stories he crafted for his own amusement. It was published posthumously by Maisie Ward. The collection includes some of Chesterton's earliest writings and comical illustrations, including a fanciful taxonomy of literary demons, caricatures of historical characters, and cartoons of himself as a disheveled figure in his idiomatic cape, gleefully eating cheese.

When I reread *The Coloured Lands,* I found most of it just as enjoyable as I had as a teen. But then there were his occasional jabs at women. And two racist drawings, of which the publisher writes: "It is regrettable that the otherwise delightful artwork of G. K. Chesterton is marred by racial caricatures. They have been retained as intrinsic to the cultural perspectives of the author and his times." But was casual racism truly intrinsic to Chesterton's times? It was systemic and widespread, to be sure, but that doesn't mean everyone was automatically racist, or equally racist. What about the many non-white residents of Britain? What about those who advocated for racial justice in that culture?

Chesterton's racism is also apparent in some of his Father
Brown stories, which feature a mystery-solving priest. Usually
either the crime or the solution showcases some sociological or
moral insight. In "The Queer Feet," the master criminal Flambeau, who later reforms and becomes Father Brown's partner
in detection, disguises himself as a waiter to steal a famous
cutlery set. The waiters assume he is one of the wealthy patrons,
and the patrons assume he is one of the waiters. At one point
a character remarks that the thief must have been very clever,
to play the role of a gentleman. "Yes," Father Brown replies, "it
must be very hard work to be a gentleman; but, do you know, I
have sometimes thought that it may be almost as laborious to
be a waiter." Another story, "The Invisible Man," also highlights
society's indifference to the working classes, as a postman nearly
gets away with murder because he is "mentally invisible."

Chesterton is at his best when addressing class issues
and lampooning the hypocrisy of the wealthy. In "The Chief
Mourner of Marne," Father Brown and some friends pay a
visit to a tortured nobleman who has been in seclusion since
murdering his friend in a duel. The nobleman's friends casti-
gate the priest for being insufficiently sympathetic to such a
tragic plight—until they learn that the nobleman killed his
friend, not in an "honorable" duel, but by trickery. Suddenly,
they are horrified. One aristocratic lady remarks that there is
a limit to human charity. Father Brown replies:

> And that is the real difference between human
> charity and Christian charity. . . . For it seems to

me that you only pardon the sins that you don't really think sinful. You only forgive criminals when they commit what you don't regard as crimes, but rather as conventions. So you tolerate a conventional duel, just as you tolerate a conventional divorce. You forgive because there isn't anything to be forgiven.[1]

Chesterton's characters are always vivid. But after a while you start to feel that these people are not quite real. They're more like types or symbols. This is especially noticeable with Chesterton's prejudices. In one story, "The Wrong Shape," Father Brown calls on a wealthy, self-involved poet who is enamored of Eastern spirituality and has a Hindu mystic as a house guest. The priest, who like his author treats all "oriental" cultures as interchangeable, detects ominous significance in the Asian and Middle Eastern artifacts in the poet's house. "The colours are intoxicatingly lovely, but the shapes are mean and bad—deliberately mean and bad," he says to Flambeau. "I have seen wicked things in a Turkey carpet."[2] What this means is never explained. It remains ominous and vague. And the mystic has nothing to do with the crime; Chesterton is just airing his prejudices.

---

[1] G. K. Chesterton, "The Chief Mourner of Marne," in *Father Brown and the Church of Rome,* ed. John Peterson (San Francisco: Ignatius Press, 1996), 38.

[2] G. K. Chesterton, "The Wrong Shape," in *The Annotated Innocence of Father Brown,* ed. Martin Gardner (Mineola, NY: Dover Publications, 1998), 143.

In "The God of the Gongs," the hidden-in-plain-sight trope gets a racist twist. At a depressing seaside resort, Father Brown and Flambeau discover that an African cult has been performing human sacrifices in broad daylight, while distracting the public as minstrels or prize fighters. The story is littered with racist commentary. In one scene, when the Black cult leader appears in evening dress, the usually likeable Flambeau says he's "not surprised that they lynch them." Father Brown replies that he is never surprised at "any work of hell." We're supposed to side with the priest, but "racially motivated murder is bad" is a pretty low bar.

Maybe the caricatures in *The Coloured Lands* arose out of the moral inadequacies of the author's culture, but Chesterton's prejudices became more intentional over time. In his novel *The Flying Inn,* xenophobia is practically the entire point. The story highlights some of the attitudes that drove the Brexit movement: love for quintessentially English things, combined with a fear of other cultures, specifically non-white ones. The narrator uses a racial slur against Black Africans on the first page, and this is followed by another caricature of another guru of vaguely Eastern antecedents.

As the story unfolds, a progressive intellectual politician falls under the influence of this guru and enforces a new Islamic regime in Britain. The conflict revolves around the sale of alcohol, which is forbidden, though the rich and powerful find ways to evade the ban. The story's protagonists, an Irish sea captain and an English pub owner, go on the run with a cask of rum and a wheel of cheese, doling out forbidden liquor, composing songs, and creating mischief, until they rally for a final battle against the Islamists and their allies.

The Flying Inn, for all its problematic notions, does lampoon the rich nicely. It also anticipates Western progressives who romanticize fundamentalist Islam, as Chesterton pokes fun at the fad of "orientalism" among the British upper classes and intelligentsia. While Chesterton has a point, in mocking artistic white people's tendency toward fetishizing all things Eastern, his view of Islam is a caricature. The plot of *The Flying Inn* also anticipates a far drearier story: French writer Michel Houellebecq's controversial novel *Submission,* in which a patriarchal, fundamentalist Muslim party takes over France with the help of the Socialists. A glum, intolerant, antireligious writer, Houellebecq seems nothing like Chesterton, yet their political views are similar. Chesterton, like Houellebecq, viewed globalism as a threat to the idealized national character. Also like Houellebecq, he regarded Islam as the apex of this threat, while obliquely admiring a perceived purity and ferocity.

While Chesterton does Islam the dubious honor of regarding it as a worthy enemy, his depictions of Jewish people are consistently dehumanizing. In a *New Yorker* essay on Houellebecq, Adam Gopnik compares him to Chesterton, noting: "For where the Jews in the European reactionary imagination are insidious termites, eating silently away at the foundations, the Muslims are outsized conquerors, arriving to take over when you're weakened. Chesterton, suspicious of Jews, was terrified of Muslims."[3] Contemporary dog whistles

---

[3] Adam Gopnik, "The Next Thing," *The New Yorker*, January 19, 2015.

about cosmopolitanism or globalism relate to Chesterton's dread of Jewish people as the sinister Other: not the enemy at the gates, but the one already here.

Despite ample evidence, many of Chesterton's fans refuse to admit to his antisemitism. "He detested racism and was an ardent opponent of racial theories, including antisemitism," the Society of G. K. Chesterton's website says. "He fought for human dignity and affirmed the brotherhood of all men"—what amounts to hagiographical fantasy. Even in his time Chesterton's antisemitism was recognized as such, and is one reason the cause for his canonization stalled in 2019. My concern is not with proving his antisemitism, but with trying to understand how it fits into his larger ideology—and why I tolerated it, despite my own Jewish heritage.

Traditionalism, localism, and prejudice

The principle now known as "Chesterton's fence" reminds us not to get rid of things without first checking to see if they are there for a reason. It's a solid argument against implementing change for its own sake. But Chesterton could have benefited from reading Shirley Jackson's "The Lottery," which warns of the opposite danger of doing things simply because they're traditional. His traditionalism sometimes borders on the reactionary, as when he mocks progressive innovations as ludicrous to anyone with common sense. Chesterton purports to showcase the absurdity of feminism, vegetarianism, even free-verse poetry, when viewed through a lens of common sense—but what he calls common sense looks more like knee-jerk resistance to anything unfamiliar, like the arguments of today's conservatives, who think they're bringing a devastating blow to "gender ideology" by loudly asserting "it's basic science that there are only two genders!" (What science actually shows is that gender is a lot more complex and fluid than many realize).

Chesterton's devotion to tradition, in itself not a bad thing, becomes a source of prejudices. The romantic image of wholesome English peasantry that he often paints is intended as a contrast not only to progressive elites but also to any outsiders or others from different cultural backgrounds who might threaten the familiar old ways.

Another good idea that Chesterton follows to an extreme is localism. Love of home, especially of one's immediate community, can be healthy and ethical, but it can also be dangerous. *The Napoleon of Notting Hill* is a charming, satirical story about a man who takes his devotion to his home neighborhood to such a fanatical degree that he raises a medieval-style army to fight off the invaders who want to run a highway through Notting Hill. It is, incidentally, a novel without a single woman character. Despite the lack of women, I loved the story when I first read it. It appeals to discontented moderns who long for an imaginary medieval world full of colors, pageantry, and traditions (just ignore the rape, death in childbirth, plague, war, and religious persecution). But the idea of defending one's home against hostile invaders, romantic as it might seem in a story, is less appealing in practice. Studies indicate that laws associated with "castle doctrine" and "stand your ground" tend to lead to an increase in rates of violence rather than deter crime.[4]

On a broader level, fascist movements have often leveraged localism to stir up animosity toward outsiders. The "blood and soil" rhetoric of the Nazis is one obvious instance of this. The MAGA movement's demonization of immigrants and refugees, a tactic that has been especially effective in rural America, is another. Less extreme examples include ecological NIMBYism, when people agitate against coal mines or landfills in their communities but are fine with them in someone else's backyard. Usually the "someone else" is a poor or marginalized community.

Both traditionalism and localism were factors that motivated the groups my family was involved in to gravitate toward the MAGA movement. At first they resisted, for obvious reasons. If you claim to value hard work, strong families, love of the land, and traditional sexual ethics, it makes no sense to support predatory, materialist, classist, corporate enrichment, and the despoiling of resources. But gradually, they began to accept, and then repeat, talking points that Trump and MAGA were touting.

---

[4] Alexa R. Yakubovich et al., "Effects of Laws Expanding Civilian Rights to Use Deadly Force in Self-Defense on Violence and Crime: A Systematic Review," *American Journal of Public Health* 111, no. 4 (April 1, 2021): e1–e14.

Our intellectual tradition, far from arming us to resist the creep of fascism, prepared us to be vulnerable to it. And Chesterton was part of that. Maybe we weren't all gung-ho for xenophobia, antisemitism, and white supremacy from the start, but we just didn't take them seriously enough. Maybe we treated Chesterton's racist ideas as mere historical quirks. Maybe we excused certain ideas because they were remarkably similar to the ideas of people we loved or respected. But the seeds of hatred took root.

"Pick me, Chesterton!"

Despite my mother being a home-schooling pioneer, we were never completely at home in those crunchy-conservative circles, partially because we were not the ideal big family ("only" three children), partially because my sister and I could never perform the traditional-woman routine in complete seriousness, partially because my father was such a loose cannon. Maybe, too, my mother's Jewishness had something to do with it. But an important fact about these communities is that they look so appealing. Imagine a big old farmhouse with friendly, attractive people in natural fibers standing around laughing and talking over beer, while someone regales them with fiddle music and adorable children run around playing. The men are quoting Chesterton. The women are cutting homemade bread. You want to belong to that. You'll even deny your identity to belong to it.

So, while I took pride in my Jewish heritage, I often tolerated, or at least laughed off, overt antisemitism. At one party a friend's husband essentially recited Mel Gibson's hate-filled paranoid screed about Jews in Hollywood, and I laughed awkwardly, because I thought I had to. The model minority gains acceptance in supremacist groups partially by accepting slurs. Ideally, repeating them. It's easy to lose your sense of identity in cultures that reward you for siding with your oppressors. If I wanted to be one of the cool Chesterton people, I had to at least not fight back.

This was the case with Chesterton's misogyny, too. Before I went to college, I'd rejected the sexism of the evangelical leaders who thought that as a woman I needed to stay in my place. Had I gone to a different school, I might have found educators who would water those seeds of feminism, but instead I entered a world where people held actual debates over whether Aristotle and Aquinas were correct to view women as misbegotten men, and where almost every authority figure was male. But how sophisticated it all seemed, compared with lowbrow bible-thumping evangelicalism. Ideas I would never have accepted from small-town preachers I willingly internalized when they were offered alongside Latin, poetry, and fine old port. It was what I had to do if I wanted to be accepted.

Even at my most conservative, however, I resented that I was offered only a few acceptable ways of being a woman, none of which suited me. I wasn't nurturing, feminine, or angelic. I was temperamental, bookish, and opinionated. Some days I tried to fit in. Other days I opted to provoke outrage by smoking cigars before class. I was looking for women role models, and though I encountered a few I admired for their intellect or strength, almost none were pursuing careers. And while my male professors encouraged me in my plans, others at that school actively discouraged women from working outside the home at all. One woman I knew dropped out of a doctoral program at an adjacent university, because the director kept sneering at her about how her only legitimate purpose there was to find a husband.

I should have responded to all this by embracing feminism. Eventually, I did. But at the time, all the intellectual heroes I looked up to were anti-feminist. Chesterton wrote about women who were strong individuals (the better to support their men), so I thought I could be like them. But all I did was become the dreaded girl who "isn't like other girls." The "pick-me" girl.

CHESTERTON'S MISOGYNY MIGHT BE subtle in his stories, but it comes through clearly in his essays. Chesterton put women on pedestals and got irked when they didn't stay there. In his view, women were not meant to seek education or careers, or to be active in politics. We are happier at home, he argued, as wives and mothers. He caricatured the entire movement of women's liberation as women trying to be like men, and the vivid women in his stories are fashioned for the male gaze. In *Divorce versus Democracy*, Chesterton opposes relaxing restrictions on divorce, even for cases of domestic violence. In his view, most women whose husbands occasionally hit them don't really mind. "She knows that while wife-beating may really be a crime, wife-hitting is sometimes very like just self-defence," he writes. "No one knows better than she does that her husband often has a great deal to put up with; sometimes she means him to; sometimes she is justified."[5]

The Society of G. K. Chesterton says we need to read these passages in context, and the context for this is Chesterton's conviction that permissive divorce laws would lead to state interference in the lives of poor families. It's a bad argument that treats women's lives as negligible—and a reminder that civilizations that praise women's fortitude while denying us equality don't value us. It's also a reminder that poisonous notions can be tucked into noble ones. Chesterton's sense of justice on behalf of the poor was real. Unfortunately, so was his misogyny. Today, conservative Christian culture rejects the first and embraces the second.

Wonder versus certainty

At age nineteen, I was confused about a lot of things, but I knew I didn't want to be meek or invisible. I wanted glory. Chesterton made me feel that I could be a bold revolutionary simply by being Catholic and assenting to traditional teachings. Maybe it's for the best that my delusions of grandeur were so easily satisfied, considering how things could have

---

[5] G. K. Chesterton, *Divorce versus Democracy*. Project Gutenberg.

gone had someone invited me to help make a crusade for Christendom a reality.

Ironically, Chesterton himself could have warned me that my seriousness about my supposed vocation was a bad sign. "Angels can fly because they take themselves lightly," he wrote in *Orthodoxy*. "Satan fell by force of gravity." This is not the first instance in which an insight from Chesterton can demolish an error in Chesterton, but that on its own is hardly an argument for keeping Chesterton in our canon. Plenty of thinkers who don't come with his baggage can offer stronger defenses. Still, even if Chesterton is a poison for some, he might be a medicine for others. But those who love him need to be wary about downplaying his dehumanizing ideologies, shaming others for being uncomfortable with blatant prejudice.

It does not seem that Chesterton grew better or wiser as his devotion to the Christian faith intensified. I like the earlier Chesterton better, Chesterton alert to the wonder and mystery of the world, curious about what lurks around corners and over hills, a little bit pagan. His conviction that he'd gotten hold of the truth made him less likable, as well as, paradoxically, less plausible. For genuine truth-seekers, every new discovery is a stepping stone. Chesterton appears to have traded curiosity and wonder for smug certainty. Maybe he decided that certainty was more comforting. His early writing conveys the uncanniness of an uncertain world. Did that trouble him? Instead of a path to mystery, did the church become a safe space to hide from it?

This is why I still love *The Man Who Was Thursday*. Unlike Chesterton's other fiction, it can't be pinned to a central message or metaphor. The plot is never fully explained. Chesterton describes the story as "a nightmare." The horror is that sometimes evil looks like good, good looks like evil, and the two are often tangled together. It's a nightmare I recognize.

4

T. S. Eliot

An apocalyptic imagination

For spring break one year, I traveled with my sister and some college friends up to Cape Ann, Massachusetts, to look at a cluster of rocks in the ocean. The rocks were not, at the time, a tourist attraction. But T. S. Eliot had named one of his Quartets after them in *The Four Quartets*, so we knew they must be important.

Today, when I google "Dry Salvages, Cape Ann," I get plenty of hits, including posts about Eliot's poem. The site has become a popular destination for literary pilgrimages, and the house in Gloucester where the young Eliot vacationed with his family is now a writer's retreat, so anyone interested in seeing the Salvages can stay there. But when we went, we had only Eliot's note: "The Dry Salvages—presumably *les trois sauvages*—is a group of rocks, with a beacon, off the N.E.

coast of Cape Ann, Massachusetts. Salvages is pronounced to rhyme with assuages."[1]

So, Cape Ann it was. We found maps, made phone calls, booked a seaside rental, and drove north. When we asked for directions in the little fishing village, the residents seemed perplexed by this gaggle of earnest college women eager to stare at some rocks best known for being a nuisance to sailors. But they pointed to where we could see the Salvages.

It was a misty, drizzly day, and even after we had clambered out on slippery stones, the object of our quest was barely visible. We made the best of it, passing around my copy of *The Complete Poems and Plays*, reading aloud in a grandiose manner. Afterward we said it had been a thrilling spiritual experience and decided to try to see the other three Quartets sites, if ever we could. The other three are located in England.

I'D BEEN TAKEN WITH Eliot's poetry since high school, partially due to his aesthetics of disillusionment—a necessary accessory for teens of my generation. But beneath my Gen X cynicism was something else, a belief that the world would soon end. This conviction, foundational to my upbringing, was a major reason for my family's countercultural lifestyle. It was why we subsisted on garden produce and lived in an abandoned farmhouse that was freezing all winter, with no running water, telephone, or television. Later I would realize

---

[1] T. S. Eliot, *The Complete Poems and Plays* (New York: Harcourt Brace and Company, 1967).

that my weird background could be a form of social capital, but as a teenager, it was embarrassing. So was my belief in the looming apocalypse. Eliot's themes of worlds ending and cities falling gave me a sophisticated way to articulate my repressed but perpetual conviction that the world was tottering toward its demise.

Eliot might have sympathized with this project of self-reinvention. By the time he was revered as the most significant modernist poet in the English language, he had spent years cultivating a brittle, grim, aloof persona. More traditionalist than the traditionalists, he disdained Oxford as gauche and considered no English monarch legitimate after Richard III. Yet Thomas Stearns Eliot was originally American, and, given his childhood in St. Louis, Missouri, might have heard a few preachers "holler" about the last judgment and the End of Days.

Eliot was the youngest in an upper-class family with roots in Boston. As a child he was plagued with poor health, forcing him to spend much of his time indoors, where he read obsessively, and began writing poetry. After completing his primary education, he studied literature at Harvard, then moved to Paris to study philosophy at the Sorbonne. When he returned to Harvard to continue his philosophical studies, he met Emily Hale, a fellow academic, with whom he fell in love. Over the course of the years Eliot would send Hale over a thousand letters, visit her, and allude to her in poems, but never propose marriage. Maybe he enjoyed the relationship more when she was always out of reach.

In 1914, as the First World War was beginning, Eliot moved to England to attend Oxford. On a trip to London he met the poet Ezra Pound, who took an interest in his work and persuaded him to marry a young woman he'd recently met, Vivienne Haigh-Wood, so he could stay in England. Eliot signed on to Pound's plan and married Haigh-Wood in 1915. Predictably, the marriage was misery for both parties. Haigh-Wood suffered from severe physical and mental health issues, and it didn't help that Eliot's upper-class, artistic friends looked down on her. In 1927, Eliot converted to Anglicanism and became a British citizen, renouncing his United States citizenship. In 1933, he and Haigh-Wood divorced. Her brother had her confined in a mental hospital, where she died in 1947. Ten years after her death Eliot, who was sixty-eight at the time, married his secretary, Esmé Valerie Fletcher, thirty-eight years his junior.

While Eliot had a long and distinguished career as a poet, he also worked as a schoolteacher, a banker, and finally in publishing, as the director of the firm now known as Faber and Faber. He died of emphysema in 1965, and his ashes were placed in St. Michael and All Angels' Church in East Coker, Somerset—a village that lends its name to one of the four Quartets.

ELIOT'S END-OF-THE-WORLD THEMES, ESPECIALLY in his earlier work, belonged to his era. He was in that group of post–World War I writers, including Gertrude Stein, Ernest Hemingway, Ezra Pound, and F. Scott Fitzgerald, now referred to as the Lost Generation, who had seen Western civilization, in all its intellectual, artistic, political, and technological glory, violently self-destruct. And when it was over, and millions were dead, no one could even say what they were fighting for. In *Hugh Selwyn Mauberley* Pound wrote about the many who died, and for what?

> For an old bitch gone in the teeth,
> For a botched civilization. . . .

So, the Lost Generation artists may have had no common vision or aesthetic creed, but all were groping in the bone yard of that "botched civilization" for some way to put their worlds together again. Pound, unfortunately, opted for fascism. He became a fan of Mussolini and ended up imprisoned as a traitor. Eliot, who shared many of Pound's views, was more refined. He chose Christianity.

Eliot's most famous poem, *The Waste Land,* reflects the geopolitical instability of the postwar era, but also Eliot's hopelessness, isolation, and physical debilitation. At the start of the 1920s, when he wrote the poem, his marriage was a disaster, and he was drinking heavily. Additionally, both he and Haigh-Wood had contracted influenza during the 1918 pandemic and been severely ill.

With the famous opening line, "April is the cruelest month," *The Waste Land* offers a sardonic nod to Chaucer's *Canterbury Tales*:

> Whan that Aprille with his shoures soote
> The droghte of March hath perced to the roote.

In Chaucer's poem, spring is the season of pilgrimages where people flirt, trade, swap tales, and all arrive at the same destination. In the Christian view, all of humanity is united in this journey toward our common end. But in Eliot's poem, there is no pilgrimage, no sense of purpose, no holy destination. Europe appears as a vast plain on which strange, isolated characters wander aimlessly, like the damned souls in Dante's hell. Images evoke fragmentation, desiccation, and death: A handful of dust. Dry bones. Mud-cracked houses. Falling towers.

The literary allusions in the poem appear as fragments, voices echoing in a wilderness. *The Waste Land* is a text about texts, inviting speculation on our relationship to texts and texts' relationships with one another. The fragments Eliot includes, whether from Augustine's *Confessions,* the poetry of Baudelaire, or bawdy music-hall tunes, are our signposts, reminding readers not where we are going, but where we came from. "These fragments I have shored against my ruins," says the ambiguous narrator, who appears in different guises throughout the poem. Sometimes he is Eliot himself; sometimes Tiresias, the blind seer from the Oedipus myth, who has lived as both a man and a woman; sometimes the Arthurian figure of the Fisher King. Imagine a survivor of a shipwreck, picking through the detritus on the shore, or an archaeologist trying to understand a lost civilization by piecing together its remnants. Eliot is archiving the artifacts of a broken world.

The fragments serve another purpose, too. *The Waste Land*'s allusions to Chaucer, Dante, and other classics of Western civilization are intended to highlight the chasm Eliot sees between past and present. Back in Chaucer's day, he implies, we understood our place in the cosmos and the social order. But that world has fallen, leaving only "fear in a handful of dust" and "a heap of broken images." Eliot, though he helped invent modernism in poetry, was a traditionalist.

Snippets of narrative appear, many depicting broken relationships. In "A Game of Chess," we get a snapshot of Eliot's miserable first marriage. In the next scene, a woman in a bar is talking about having an affair with her friend's husband. There is an allusion to the myth of Procne and Philomel, which tells of betrayal, rape, and cannibalism. We see an unpleasant man seducing a bored woman. These shattered relationships, a microcosm of Western civilization, are sterile. There are no children in "A Game of Chess." The woman in the bar gossips about her friend taking abortion pills. At one point, the narrator is accosted by "Mr. Eugenides, the Smyrna merchant," who invites him to "a weekend at the Metropole." People meet for loveless sex, but no one reproduces. We hear "Murmur of maternal lamentation," Rachel weeping for her children. The only living children are "bats with baby faces." The land is dry and barren, and so are human loves. Things are not what they were.

IN COLLEGE, WE LOOKED at Eliot through a culture-war lens, which meant ignoring historical context. Instead of considering that Eliot had just seen millions die in a senseless war, then millions more in a pandemic, we focused on his dislike of modernity. We saw the Europe of *The Waste Land* as a cautionary tale about a secular culture destroyed by globalism and pluralism, relationships destroyed by contraception and homosexuality. Probably Eliot would not hate every aspect of this interpretation, but it's not, fundamentally, what the poem is about. You can't understand *The Waste Land* without recognizing one of its themes: that traditional Western civilization brought about its own demise. Yet *The Waste Land* is not completely hopeless. At its close, the narrator sits with the arid plain in the background, fishing. The narrator might be the Fisher King, but the scene also echoes Peter in the Gospels. "Shall I at least set my lands in order?" the writer asks. The final word of the poem—*shantih*, repeated three times—is the formal ending to an Upanishad and, Eliot explains in his notes, means "the peace that passeth understanding" in Sanskrit.

"We had the experience but missed the meaning"

If *The Waste Land* is the saga of the lost, Eliot's *Ash Wednesday* offers a promise of redemption. It is a poem of retrospection, acceptance, and calmness after sorrow. The opening ("Because I do not hope to turn again") echoes the first line of medieval Florentine poet Guido Cavalcanti's poem on his exile: "Because I do not hope ever to return." Emptiness and hopelessness are not the final word, but reasons to change your life. Even fragmentation becomes a blessing, since the old life was bad and needed to be taken apart. Now maybe something better can grow.

The poem alludes to the fairy tale "The Juniper Tree"— a story about murder and cannibalism, echoing Procne and Philomel—but, in *Ash Wednesday*, being eaten is not so bad. The bones scattered under the tree are happy about it: "We are glad to be scattered, we did little good to each other." The cyclical movement of *The Waste Land* is reiterated, but here it's not pointless. Ascending a spiral staircase, there is a clearer vista the higher the speaker goes.

By the time we get to *The Four Quartets*, Eliot's relationship with the fragments archived in memory has shifted. The turn toward memory is a turn toward understanding. Each of the mixed-format poems—*Burnt Norton, East Coker, The Dry Salvages*, and *Little Gidding*—is named for a place Eliot considered significant in his life, and each reflects one of the four elements. Eliot composed the four poems over a six-year period, between 1936 and 1942, and ultimately intended the collection to be treated as a complete work. Many, including Eliot himself, regard *The Four Quartets* as his poetic masterpiece.

One professor at my university categorized Eliot's poetry according to the three parts of Dante's *Divine Comedy*. According to this view *The Waste Land*, written before Eliot became Christian, is infernal. *Ash Wednesday*, written after his conversion, is purgatorial. And *The Four Quartets* is Eliot's *Paradiso.* This approach works, up to a point. Eliot drew heavily on *The Divine Comedy,* and his writing changed after his conversion. Other writers of his time remarked on it. Some, put off by the overtly religious themes and language, thought he'd departed too much from his earlier style. Eliot's conversion was a subject of general disapproval in his literary circles. Virginia Woolf, a close friend of his, wrote in a 1928 letter to her sister that his conversion "shocked" her.

From a culture-war perspective, Eliot was the righteous one, striking out on his own for truth and goodness, while the rest of the Lost Generation remained lost. In graduate school I remember one of my peers talking about Woolf's death from suicide as though it proved something about her beliefs—as though it had nothing to do with surviving sexual abuse and dealing with mental illness. But Eliot despaired too. And, as poet and essayist Christian Wiman writes of Woolf, "Her despair and Eliot's were facets of the same thing."[2] Why one person survives the valley of the shadow, and another doesn't, is often a matter of chance, not creed.

EVENTUALLY I MADE IT to the other three Quartet sites. A few years after our quest for the Dry Salvages, my sister and I, along with our mother and one friend from the original quest, visited Burnt Norton, a manor house near Chipping

---

[2] Christian Wiman, *Zero at the Bone: Fifty Entries against Despair* (New York: Farrar, Straus, and Giroux, 2023), 59.

Campden in Gloucestershire, in the Cotswolds region of England. It came by its name after a baronet who resided there in the eighteenth century drunkenly set himself, and the entire house, on fire. He did not survive. The house was later rebuilt, and in 1935 Eliot visited Emily Hale there. This visit inspired the first of the Quartets.

The manor was easier to find than the Dry Salvages. Once again, it was March. The rose garden, an important detail in the poem, was sleeping, and we walked quietly down the dry paths, each on our own, before gathering by a bare garden plot to read aloud. *Burnt Norton*'s element is air, and its images conjure the calm of a summer evening filled with memories, hidden presences, something important or someone beloved, just out of reach.

A theme in *The Four Quartets* is that we continue to return to powerful moments in our memories, attempting to make sense of them. "Human kind can not bear very much reality," Eliot writes in *Burnt Norton*. Then, in *The Dry Salvages*, "We had the experience but missed the meaning."

So what can I find now, in my memories of those visits? The year I went to Burnt Norton I was pursuing the PhD in literature. I was confident and hopeful, looking toward the future. Little did I know I was about to make a series of terrible decisions, and tumble into my own personal waste land. Now, rereading *Burnt Norton*, I stop at these lines:

What might have been and what has been
Point to one end, which is always present.

Whatever the past may have been, the present is what we have.

Shortly after that trip, my life fell apart. I was offered a job at a new liberal-arts college and unadvisedly took it. Since I was trying to extricate myself from a toxic and damaging relationship, getting away seemed like a good idea, though this meant I'd be trying to master classical Latin and complete my dissertation while teaching full time. Things did not go well. The new college turned out to be even more bizarre and regressive than the one I had attended as an undergraduate, and I found myself constantly battling the administration, challenging its punitive measures against students who stepped out of line even a little. But I was starting to unravel. After years of pushing myself to excel, the stress of that work environment combined with heartbreak and self-loathing took its toll. Within a year, I went from promising academic to hard-partying bartender. I think I was trying to punish myself.

It took me years to claw myself out of that moral, psychological, and financial hole, but finally I reinvented myself—again. I moved back to where my parents lived, and started teaching philosophy and literature at my not-so-alma mater. Any illusions I'd had about that place were long gone, but I was excited to be teaching again, and this time I was good at it. Over the years I got to know many thoughtful, witty, courageous, empathetic, and sometimes brilliant young people whose questions and observations challenged me to expand my own horizons. Every semester I revised my courses to account for new ideas that had come up in class discussion.

I learned other things from my students, too. Sometimes, after class, a student would wait to talk to me, and tell me about something unsettling that had happened. Male professors making creepy remarks to young women. Assault survivors who had gotten no help from student life. LGBTQ+ students who had been warned by their RAs not to come out. Later I learned that queer students exchanged notes about which staff or faculty members were safe to come out to. Over the years, that number dwindled, as non-conservative instructors left, or were fired.

At the time, I didn't understand the connections between my phase of far-right Christianity and my phase of self-destruction. I thought that the ideology I'd embraced as an undergraduate, though quaint and silly, was fundamentally harmless. Hearing from my students about their experiences, I began to question this. Stories began to circulate about campus priests abusing students and university administrators covering this up. Unable to pretend anymore that conservative ideologies were harmless, I decided to assign more controversial material in classes. I began writing about women's rights and criticized the politically motivated and mixed ethics of the pro-life movement that privileged one distinct form of life, while devaluing the lives of mothers, the lives of the poor and the marginalized, and disregarding the profound complexity of many women's lived experiences and situations.

But I still wasn't prepared for 2016. I wasn't prepared for so many of the people I'd respected for years, even some of my closest friends, to support the MAGA movement. Had I never really known them? And how had all our talk about truth, beauty, and goodness led to this?

The right good old way

In 2016 I also picked up the long-abandoned thread of our Eliot pilgrimage. Finally financially secure enough to travel again, I flew to England to spend a week with my sister, and we drove to St. John's Church in the village of Little Gidding in Cambridgeshire, the site of the Anglican community where King Charles I sought refuge in 1646. The final poem in the Quartets, *Little Gidding,* was inspired by Eliot's 1936 visit to the tiny church in its peaceful green yard, filled with slanting old stones.

On our journey, we discussed the respective issues in our nations, Trump in the US and Brexit in the UK. We understood that propaganda was a factor, and that people who'd had fewer educational opportunities might be manipulated into supporting xenophobic movements, but what about our educated, cultivated friends? Including some who'd been on our original Eliot quest? It made no sense.

In the little church, I knelt by a modest stained-glass window bearing the words, "IT IS THE RIGHT GOOD OLD WAY

YOU ARE IN. KEEP IN IT." I thought about Eliot's search for connection in a world of change and uncertainty. I thought about the "broken king" arriving at the church at night. As we read aloud from the poem, a deep tranquility came over me. "All shall be well," Eliot writes, quoting Julian of Norwich. "And all manner of thing shall be well." The universe, I thought, is larger than I can imagine. Perhaps there is a vaster order here, beyond what I can comprehend. The final stanza reads:

> We shall not cease from exploration
> And the end of all our exploring
> Will be to arrive where we started.

We completed our Four Quartets quest two years later. On a sunny spring day, my sister and I arrived at the Church of St. Michael and All Angels' Church in East Coker. Once again, we read aloud from the poem, far less reverentially than we had the first two times. How insufferable we must have been in our youth. How silly we were in our middle years, reclining dramatically upon gravestones, no longer worried about cultivating an aura of sophistication. As Eliot knew, either way you come to dust in the end. We walked around the church, stopping at the plaque where Eliot's ashes reposed. Here he was at last, the old guy. What would he make of the world that had gone on without him? What would he think about his fanboys who prayed in Latin in the mornings, then applauded the incarceration of immigrant children in the afternoon? I muttered some choice words to him, there in the quiet church.

But I was beginning to find answers to some of the questions that had perplexed me two years before. On one level, it made no sense for people who love art and beauty to support a far-right populist movement predicated on hate. On the other hand, maybe this was the logical outcome of the culture-war thinking I too had embraced in early adulthood: to wander from the "right good old way" right into fascism.

Christianity ought to militate against this. The gospel message has one of the strongest possible antidotes to fascism, yet somehow, the church has often sided with fascists. Eliot, however, did not join Pound in taking that route, maybe because fascism has no space for those who suffer. The fascist hero must always be victorious, but Christianity makes space for those who are wounded or oppressed. I think Eliot understood this. In *The Idea of a Christian Society*, he argues that England needed to return to a Christian ordering of society. Even if he is vague about how this would work, he does seem to hold that in such a society, radical inequities should be eliminated. Unfortunately, many of his views—tradition as magisterial, the past as preferable, and modernity as debased—fit a little too neatly into a fascist toolkit.

Still, Eliot's poetry rises above this. The story it tells is a lot like religious deconstruction. *The Waste Land* and its fragments speak to my experience of sorting through the rubble of my old beliefs, trying to decide what's worth keeping. Like the speaker in *Ash Wednesday,* I try to see this as a blessing. Maybe I will rise above the mess of my past and find a second chance. So I carry on, down the corridors of memory, searching for whatever it was I missed the first time around.

5

Dorothy Sayers

The way things might have been

An intellectual young woman returns to the college where she was once a promising scholar before she made some regrettable decisions and got embroiled in a scandal. At first, she worries her former teachers and peers will look askance at her, because of her notoriety. For the most part, they don't, but going back evokes memories both painful and poignant. Now a successful writer, she takes pride in her independence, but wonders about the life she could have had in this ordered and tranquil academic refuge. But she soon learns, the refuge isn't so tranquil after all. As she begins investigating a series of escalating pranks, she is drawn into a web of secrets, scandals, and crimes.

This is the premise of Dorothy Sayers's novel *Gaudy Night,* one of her Lord Peter Wimsey mysteries. When I read it as a young academic woman, it felt validating. Sayers was one of the "good guys," on the list of the approved Christian writers, and here she was offering thoughtful critiques of traditionalist views on marriage, work, and gender roles. Though I was confronted daily with sexist biases, I had been conditioned to reject feminism and was hesitant to identify with a movement my entire subculture scorned. Sayers gave me a license to discuss women's rights and the stupidity of traditionalist gender roles—albeit in an oblique manner.

Revisiting *Gaudy Night* years later, it felt relatable in a different way. In terms of feminism, I'd traveled far beyond Sayers's tentative forays. But her reflections on life choices and vocation felt achingly relevant. I kept wondering how my life might have gone if I'd attended a different school, started questioning sooner, discovered more liberating views on sex and gender. What if I'd understood earlier that a woman doesn't need to be in a romantic relationship to have a meaningful life? What if I hadn't beat myself up for things that weren't my fault? How might I have been happier, stronger, a better person, less messed up?

Since the story is about academia, it was especially evocative reading it that second time around. At one point I read the words aloud: "They can't take this away, at any rate. Whatever I may have done since, this remains. Scholar, Master of Arts . . . a place achieved, inalienable, worthy of reverence."[1] Reading her words I had an image of a younger

---

[1] Dorothy Sayers, *Gaudy Night* (New York: HarperPaperbacks, 1995), 8.

version of myself, confident, fashionable, presenting a paper on Plato's views on poetry at a graduate conference. After my talk, several professors told me it was the best interpretation of the topic they'd ever heard. We were drinking wine. Some flirtation was happening. For a little while I was on top of my little world.

GAUDY NIGHT'S RELATABILITY LASTS only up to a point. Sayers's protagonist, Harriet Vane, attended an (imaginary) college at Oxford, not a second-rate conservative university in the United States. The community she returns to may be insular, but it is vibrant, and serious about scholarship. The scholars value Harriet as a person and professional and ask her help in solving the mystery. And Harriet's college, for all its imperfections, has not been complicit in ongoing sex-abuse coverups.

Then Harriet's brilliant, eccentric, aristocratic admirer, Lord Peter Wimsey, appears on the scene to assist in the investigations, and the detective story becomes a romance, with idyllic Oxford as the backdrop. I never had an aristocratic admirer show up to help me solve campus mysteries, but my toxic love interest from graduate-school days resembled Lord Peter in certain ways. Behaving honorably with women was not one of them.

Though Peter is persistent in his pursuit of Harriet, he is also respectful of her space and her wishes. So Harriet has two enigmas to solve: One, who is persecuting women academics with nasty letters and acts of vandalism? Two, how does she feel about Peter? Connected with that is the question of whether she can balance the life of the mind with the possibility of romance and marriage. She and the women scholars discuss the importance of work (something Sayers took seriously) and the pressures placed on women to conform to society's demands. But as the pranks get more violent, the women begin to turn on one another.

The women scholars are aware that their patriarchal culture refuses to take them seriously, aware of the cruel jokes about frustrated virgins who just need men in their lives. This makes the tension among them especially fraught. However (spoiler alert), the perpetrator of the crimes is not an academic. She's a housekeeper with a secret vendetta against professional women ever since her late husband, a scholar, died of suicide after his female colleague exposed him as an academic fraud. Throughout most of the story she is a background character, a foil to the independent women scholars, with her fervent traditionalism. Not until the denouement is it clear how deeply this nice, conventional wife and mother hates career women, especially academic career women. In *Gaudy Night,* as in real life, obsession with strict gender roles can lead to gender violence, and women who embrace patriarchy can be the most vitriolic in their defense of it.

THE VENGEFUL HOUSEKEEPER'S OPINIONS were not new to me, but I was surprised to find Sayers plainly depicting them as harmful. Yet Sayers was not, strictly speaking, a feminist. In her memorable 1938 lecture titled "Are Women Human?"

she declined to identify with the movement, saying she thought the time for feminism had passed. Nevertheless, she took feminist positions out of exasperation with a patriarchal world that refused to see women as individuals. In a *New Yorker* essay on *Gaudy Night*, Nora Caplan-Bricker writes that "Sayers's most cherished feminist commitment is that our true selves are tied up in our talents: that every person, regardless of gender, has a type of work for which they're intrinsically suited, and that the ethical choice in life is, as Harriet says, to 'do one's own job, however trivial.'"[2]

A woman of character

Sayers is hard to pin down, and not just on questions of women's rights. It makes sense that she would resist efforts to box women in, given how staunchly individual she was. She's been accused of antisemitism, yet her views on the Jewish people are completely unlike Chesterton's, and sometimes even seem favorable. Her relationship to religion is also difficult to categorize: She was impatient with sentimental, pietistic, low-church Christianity, but her faith was important to her, and in her later years she shifted from writing crime stories to writing Christian apologetics.

---

[2] Nora Caplan-Bricker, "An Overlooked Novel from 1935, by the Godmother of Feminist Detective Fiction," *The New Yorker*, November 13, 2019.

The daughter of a rector, Sayers was born in 1893 and grew up in a small village in East Anglia. She was educated largely at home, with few social opportunities but lots of time for reading. She seems to have been the kind of strong-minded, free-thinking, home-schooled person I remember from my parents' long-ago artsy social circle, before we got sucked into conservative Christian communities that prioritized obedience and conformity. Dorothy, in her teens, eventually attended a boarding school, but it wasn't a good fit; she was too independent for the school, and the school was too pious for Sayers.

She attended Oxford at a time when few women were admitted. While there, she and several other women students founded a literary group, the Mutual Admiration Society (the name was intended ironically, to stave off mockery from the male students). When she graduated in 1915, she wasn't permitted to take a degree, despite her first-class honors. Five years later, the university changed its policies, and Sayers became one of the first women to receive an Oxford degree.

Prior to writing mystery stories, Sayers worked as a teacher, as a publisher, and in an ad agency. Her first novel, *Whose Body?* introduced Lord Peter Wimsey. She would go on to write eleven novels and twenty-one short stories featuring Wimsey and become successful enough as a crime writer to quit her job in advertising. Later she moved away from detective fiction to pursue "serious" writing: plays, poems, essays, and translations. Sayers, like her creation Harriet, did worry that writing about murder for a popular audience was an insufficiently serious vocation. But she had no Lord Peter to assure her that her work was important.

Wimsey, with his beakish nose, vapid expressions, and tendency to babble erudite nonsense, is far from stereotypically "hot," but that is part of his charm. Of course, he's also fantastically athletic, stupendously well-read, and a favorite with society ladies. If Sayers sometimes seems in love with her own creation, this is unsurprising, since she based his appearance and mannerisms on several men for whom she suffered unrequited longings, including the writer Roy Ridley, with whom she studied at Oxford.

Though Sayers never found romance with Ridley, she did have an intense relationship with the writer John Cournos. It was not a happy affair. She wanted marriage and children. He wanted free love. Since she refused to use birth control for religious reasons, their relationship was never sexually consummated. We get a glimpse into Sayers and Cournos's unfulfilling romance in the novel *Strong Poison,* which introduces Harriet Vane, on trial for murdering her former lover. Harriet's unhappy cohabitation with her deceased ex was based on Sayers's toxic romance with Cournos. Despite her austere tastes and lofty principles, Sayers wasn't above writing wish-fulfillment fantasy or revenge fiction.

After her romance with Cournos ended, Sayers had a brief affair with a man who turned out to be married. She became pregnant, and had a son, who was raised by a close friend. In 1926, Sayers married a journalist, Oswald Arthur Fleming. This, too, was not an ideal union. She was the primary breadwinner, but Fleming, who was inclined to drink heavily and neglect his work, resented her success. It's easy to imagine Sayers retreating into the fictional world she'd created, and into the company of Lord Peter, who would understand her literary references, appreciate her artistry, and respect her writing.

Like Chesterton, Sayers was a recognizable and eccentric figure in her day. She dressed dramatically, smoked cigars, and cultivated a masculine aesthetic. She and Chesterton were friends, and when she co-founded the Detection Club, a literary group for mystery writers, he was made president.

Around the late 1930s, Sayers began to shift her focus from detective stories to more overtly religious writing, including plays and essays. In the last decade of her life, she was occupied, even obsessed, with translating Dante's *Divine Comedy* into English. At the time of her death of heart failure in 1957, she had published translations of *Inferno* and *Purgatorio* and was about halfway through her work on *Paradiso*. Her *Inferno* was a bestseller when it came out, but many readers today find it unsatisfactory due to her attempt to render Dante's *terza rima* in English; trying to imitate the rhyme scheme of the original made for some awkward or inaccurate work.

A template for prejudice

Perhaps Sayers was trying to recreate herself as a serious and scholarly writer, putting her time with Lord Peter behind her.

Nevertheless, she's best remembered for her mysteries. She is also frequently thought of as a kind of unofficial member of the Inklings, the all-male literary group that included Lewis and Tolkien. But though Sayers was a serious Christian, this doesn't come through much in her popular writing—neither overtly, like Chesterton, nor covertly, like Flannery O'Connor. Sayers resides firmly within the detective genre, including within its established social codes—even when she critiques them.

And she does critique them, up to a point. Many of Sayers's characters say and do racist things, which is unsurprising, given that British racism in the era she describes, between the two world wars, became especially intense and ugly. For years, Britain had spread its imperial web, occupying nations, stealing their treasures, appropriating their traditions. Then, during World War I, workers from West Africa, the West Indies, Somalia, and other colonized lands moved to England to aid in military and manufacturing efforts. Then they stayed on, working in industry, but many in the white population, especially soldiers returning from the war, resented them. Riots broke out. White mobs attacked the lodgings of Black workers. The police usually sided with the white perpetrators. At the same time, as some non-white workers began marrying white English women, an anti-miscegenation movement began. This background is important for understanding racial references in the literature of 1920s England. It's not just "thoughtless" prejudice. As in the Jim Crow era in the United States, the racist rhetoric of this time is a symptom of a larger movement of aggressive hate.

Sayers, with her close attention to craft, did not write her racist characters casually. The nastiest comments usually come from characters we're not supposed to view favorably. In the novel *Unnatural Death,* gossipy women make rude assumptions about a Black clergyman who is distantly related to the murder victim. The women are presented as unpleasant and a little ridiculous, the clergyman as a sympathetic and dignified figure. When the murderer herself attempts to cast suspicion on him, the reader is invited to compare his moral character with hers. Laura Vorachek, in an article for *Clues: A Journal of Detection,* argues that this plot detail in *Unnatural Death* "attempts to counter associations of blackness with criminality that are found in many contemporary crime narratives by demonstrating how that assumption can be manipulated and by critiquing those who accept the correlation as fact."[3]

But Sayers's critiques of racism are not exactly bold. And her representation of the clergyman as mild-mannered and docile recapitulates white racist notions about the "right kind" of Black man. Nevertheless, Sayers's willingness to criticize racism is a reminder that we can't exonerate Chesterton by arguing that "everyone thought that way back then." As a middle-class white intellectual, Sayers may not offer the best arguments against racism, but she's moving in the right direction.

---

[3] Laura Vorachek, "His Appearance Is against Him": Race and Criminality in Dorothy L. Sayers's *Unnatural Death,*" *Clues: A Journal of Detection* 37, no. 2 (Fall 2019): 61–70.

BUT THEN THERE'S THE matter of antisemitism. Jews show up a lot in Sayers's stories, often in stereotypical roles, as financiers or moneylenders. Yet her Jewish characters seem less like caricatures than her working-class characters, and they are usually portrayed sympathetically.

In her first Peter Wimsey novel, the mystery revolves around an unidentified naked body found in a bath, initially assumed to be that of an eminent (and ethical) Jewish financier, who has vanished mysteriously. Lord Peter shows up and notes that the dead man is not the missing financier. Sayers doesn't say so directly, but the obvious clue is that the man is uncircumcised, and so can't be Jewish. The body in the bathtub is a red herring, placed there by the murderer, a celebrated doctor who was once a romantic rival to the financier—whom he has indeed killed. Similarly to how she contrasted the Black clergyman with the vapid, mean-spirited white women, Sayers's depiction of the doctor as an amoral sociopath invites comparison with the moral uprightness of his victim. Later, in *Strong Poison,* Peter's good friend Freddy Arbuthnot falls in love with the daughter of the murdered financier. They marry in a synagogue, with Lord Peter as a witness, and plan to raise their children Jewish.

Other Jews show up on occasion, usually presented as attractive, thoughtful people. If we take Sayers at her word, she intended to portray her Jewish characters in a positive light; when some critics pointed to possible antisemitism in *Whose Body,* she claimed that actually the Jews were the only people presented favorably in the story. We don't have to take her word for it, since she's hardly in a position to say what is or isn't antisemitic, but if she really meant to portray her Jewish characters positively, this is intriguing.

Amy E. Schwartz, in an essay in *Moment* (a publication dedicated to Jewish thought, founded by Elie Wiesel and activist Leonard Fein), notes the recurrence of Jewish characters in Sayers's stories. "Just how did the celebrated detective novelist actually feel about her Jewish characters?" she asks. "And why, in these books, can't she seem to shut up about them? Why are there so many? Something is going on, something more complicated and personal than casual anti-Semitism and a good deal more interesting."[4]

Schwartz proposes a theory. She calls attention to the Jewishness of Sayers's difficult first lover, John Cournos, born Ivan Grigorievich Korshun in present-day Ukraine. Sayers wrote a novel about the murdered Jewish man while in a relationship with a Jewish man. Was Sayers's fraught relationship with Cournos at the root of her fixation on the Jewish people? Was there a little writerly revenge going on, as well? But she chose to make the dead Jewish man virtuous, with a happy family life. Perhaps Sayers was thinking about what could have been.

Whatever Sayers's motives, *Strong Poison* was written in 1931. Fourteen years later, in an essay about the future of the Jews in England, Sayers advanced a not very original thesis

---

[4] Amy E. Schwartz, "The Curious Case of Dorothy L. Sayers and the Jew Who Wasn't There," *Moment Magazine*, July-August 2016.

about Judaism. She claimed that the coming of Christ had been "the turning-point of human history" and that the Jews had "missed that turning-point and got stranded." Quite a claim to make, immediately after the murder of six million Jews in the Second World War—even if Sayers, at the time, wasn't yet aware of the extent of the Holocaust. Her argument reads like a variation on supersessionism: the idea that God's new covenant, through Christ, has erased and replaced God's covenant with the Jewish people. It's worth noting that the real reason Jews have suffered repeatedly in the centuries after Christ is not because they "missed the turning-point" or "lost divine favor" or "killed Christ." It's because of widespread antisemitism—the seeds of which lie in the early church, and which Christianity tended and kept alive through the centuries.

If Sayers had been able to think more intelligently about the Jews and Judaism, would she have separated them from her emotions about Cournos? How would she have felt about the Jewish people had she not had a dysfunctional relationship with a Jewish man? And how much of her embrace of Christian antisemitism, in the form of supersessionism, was informed by her resentment of Cournos? Whatever the case, her prejudices against the Jews appear to have been exacerbated, not diminished, as she became more invested in her Christian faith. It is possible that Christianity, with its ready-made anti-Jewish narratives, gave her a template for presenting her prejudices as intellectually and doctrinally honorable.

Class and Christianity

Not that Sayers leaned into her Christianity to spite Cournos or anyone. Her faith practice was sincere and carefully thought out. Based on what we know about her unconsummated relationship with Cournos, she was willing to suffer to stick with her principles. When her play *The Man Born to Be King* scandalized the pious, she was not perturbed and may even have enjoyed causing consternation. She was not a woman to be bullied into conformity, and she had little interest in a religion of rules and platitudes. Sayers wanted her Christianity challenging, even intellectually thrilling, and she was serious about trying to understand the historical Jesus.

But what did Sayers understand Christian values to be? Her refusal to let Cournos bully her into doing something she felt uncomfortable about is commendable. Nonetheless, even though people broadly associate prohibitions on birth control with Christianity, especially Catholic Christianity, it's hardly a core gospel value.

The actual gospel values of justice, the preferential option for the poor, and radical love of neighbor don't really seem to come into Sayers's writing. If they did, this might make things uncomfortable for Lord Peter. What would Jesus say about his rare books, fast cars, and fine wine? Wimsey has a good bit of class guilt, and one reason he solves crimes is because he feels he owes it to society to not be a useless parasite. But he doesn't seem troubled about gospel teachings about wealth and poverty; it's more a matter of masculine pride.

Certainly, Christianity did not compel Sayers to reject her class prejudices. Her working-class characters are usually comic caricatures, complete with dialect and uncouth mannerisms. Lord Peter is great at connecting with the commoners, but this comes off as just another aristocratic skill, like being good with horses. While Lord Peter and Harriet are people, sensitive and complex, the working-class people around them often seem to lack interiority. As for radicals and reformers, she paints them as rather vulgar, largely unnecessary, and a bit ridiculous.

All this makes Sayers's talk about Christianity's excitement, and her willingness to shock the pious, seem tame, a purely intellectual adventure that doesn't affect the social order. In her fiction, at any rate, it evokes a very English respectability: vicars, the village church, and Lord Peter singing in the choir at Christmas. The Christian code appears, but it's a pale, timid sort of thing, always subsumed into a broader social code that has little to do with Jesus's teachings.

Perhaps the most obvious instance of this is at the end of the novel *The Unpleasantness at the Bellona Club*. Wimsey, having solved the mystery, quietly confronts the perpetrator and implies that his best bet, to avoid scandal and disgrace, is to kill himself. From a Christian perspective, a moral horror. From the perspective of the gentlemanly code, perfectly acceptable. It's another variation on white middle-class writers mistaking Western Christendom with Christianity itself.

Peter leaves the man alone in a room with a pistol. A little later, the sound of a gunshot is heard throughout the opulent chambers of the club.

6

Evelyn Waugh

I was happy once, too

The first time I taught *Brideshead Revisited*, I fed my students the same interpretation my professors had given me. This, I said, is a story about people driven by a yearning to fill their own emptiness, not yet knowing that God is seeking them, even through their most debased desires. When they are drawn to love, that's God. When they lose that love, that's God too. Every joy and heartbreak is the twitch upon the thread with which God draws the errant sinner back to grace.

Evelyn Waugh's most famous novel opens with the protagonist, Charles Ryder, in his middle years, serving as an army captain during World War II, in a condition of dreary disillusionment. The descriptions of army life here and in Waugh's *Sword of Honor* trilogy are modeled on the author's own wartime experiences. Fiercely conservative, Waugh was ready to be enthusiastic about imaginary crusader battles but couldn't stomach the bureaucratic realities of military logistics.

You can probably deduce a bit about Waugh from the fact that he saw the Allied and Axis powers as largely equivalent and supported Mussolini's brutal treatment of Ethiopia. He was racist and antisemitic. At Oxford, he had sexual relationships with other men but treated them as a passing phase, a prelude to heterosexual romance. He drank heavily and self-medicated with drugs. He claimed to have attempted suicide by drowning himself in the ocean, only to be deterred by an attack of jellyfish—but this story may have been fabricated. When he began making money, he evaded taxes by setting up a trust fund for his own kids called the Save the Children fund. Then there's the infamous banana story, recounted by his son Auberon: During wartime rationing, the family got a hold of three bananas, intended for the children. Waugh sliced them, covered them with cream and sugar, and ate them while his children looked sadly on. I am aware of no evidence that he ever felt guilty about this. Waugh was a brilliant writer, but not a nice man.

He wrote *Brideshead Revisited* while on military leave in 1944 and nostalgic for the opulence of prewar times. "It was a bleak period of present privation and threatening disaster—the period of soya beans and Basic English—and in consequence, the book is infused with a kind of gluttony for food and wine, for the splendors of the recent past, and for rhetorical and ornamental language," Waugh wrote in the preface to the revised edition. The book is not only inspired by nostalgia; it is about nostalgia. The subtitle is *The Sacred and Profane Memories of Captain Charles Ryder*, and the narrative that unfolds is made up largely of Charles's recollections. "My theme is memory," he says at the opening of Book II, "that winged host that soared about me one grey morning of war-time. These memories, which are my life—for we possess nothing certainly except the past—were always with me."[1]

The framing device for the novel is Charles discovering that his company has been posted at the country estate where he spent the most important years of his life, first as a student, later in his prime. Here he twice found love, and twice lost it. *"Et in Arcadia Ego,"* is the title of Book I, alluding to the mythic realm of Arcadia, a place of beauty and harmony with nature. The phrase appears in the second chapter, inscribed on a skull that rests in a bowl of roses in Charles's Oxford rooms, once he has embraced the fashions of an aesthete. It can be read as "I was happy once, too." Or as "even in Arcadia, I, death, am present." Either way, it's ominous.

The first part of the book focuses on the Arcadian years, in which the charming Sebastian Flyte draws Charles out of his bland, respectable Oxford life into his circle of upper-class aesthetes, then invites him to stay at his family's majestic home. For a time, the two are inseparable and enjoy an enchanted existence in a world of their own dreamy making. They drink wine, stroll in the gardens, play games,

---

[1] Evelyn Waugh, *Brideshead Revisited* (New York: Little, Brown, and Company, 1999), 225.

dabble in art, and the subtext suggests, engage in erotic intimacy. Sebastian seems bothered by his family, though, and Charles can't understand why, since he finds them delightful: Lady Marchmain with her wide-eyed charm, the fashionable older sister, Julia, the mischievous but devout younger sister, Cordelia, and the old-fashioned oldest brother, Bridey, heir to the estate. Sebastian's parents are estranged, and his father, who'd become Catholic in order to marry, has left the church and now lives in Italy with his mistress. Charles's primary concern is being with Sebastian, however, and for a short time, he knows happiness.

Waugh's descriptions of the golden days of youth and languor are so evocative, readers feel they have lived them themselves: Plovers' eggs at tea, the flamboyant Anthony Blanche reciting T.S. Eliot through a megaphone, strawberries and Château Peyraguey in an elm grove. I've read accounts of Americans who, spending time at Oxford, tried to recreate Waugh's scenes. In graduate school I was friends with a man who went through a phase of carrying a teddy bear around campus, as Sebastian does. My sister and I, along with a few of our friends, tried to cosplay Brideshead people at our grimy little campus under a sky that smelled perpetually of rotten eggs. Waugh, an inveterate snob, inadvertently inspired a trend of people attempting to be flamboyant and sophisticated but only coming off as ridiculous.

But I still have nostalgia for our lunch breaks under a single sad dogwood tree, surreptitiously swigging Carlo Rossi burgundy out of plastic cups. If no one will make the magic for you, you can make it for yourself, even idiotically. And somehow, I saw no contradiction between attempting (badly, of course) to ape the modes of decadent 1920s aesthetes while also upholding conservative ideologies. But I suppose Waugh didn't, either. And I can't call it hypocrisy, because he wasn't even pretending to be ethical.

The church of the elite

Arthur Evelyn St. John Waugh, known as Evelyn, came from a solidly middle-class family, but cultivated high-society tastes—even delusions of grandeur. Socially and academically successful from a young age, he was a bully in his prep school days—and continued to be one throughout his life.

Originally Waugh planned to attend the prestigious public school Sherborne, but then his older brother Alec caused a scandal by writing a novel based on his experience of being kicked out of that school for being in a gay relationship. So Evelyn went, instead, to Lancing College, where he excelled academically and won a scholarship to Hertford College, Oxford. There, he was drawn into an upper-class avant-garde circle that later inspired his description both of London's Bright Young Things, and of Charles's Oxford set, complete with heavy drinking and sexual adventures. After his promising academic start, Waugh neglected his studies, lost his scholarship, and had to leave without completing his degree.

For a time, Waugh dabbled ingloriously in teaching, journalism, carpentry, and printing. But he kept on writing, and he published his first novel, *Decline and Fall*, in 1928, to favorable reviews. That same year he married his first wife, the socialite Evelyn Gardner. They were known as He-Evelyn and She-Evelyn. A little over a year into their marriage, She-Evelyn had an affair with one of their friends, and the two split up, leaving Waugh bitter and disillusioned. His novel *Vile Bodies* (1930) reflects his mood at the time. That novel, as well as *Decline and Fall* and later *A Handful of Dust*, implements a motif of futility, aimless people cycling through the same patterns, always ending up in the same place, always the same people reappearing.

Waugh's many serious moral and ideological flaws did not impede his genius, especially when it came to capturing humanity's most dismal attributes. Maybe his depression gave him insight into our fundamental cussedness, the thing Christians call original sin. And maybe that's why, despite years of indifference to religion, he decided to convert to Catholicism around the time his first marriage fell apart. While his conversion was largely intellectually motivated, it was also, apparently, sincere. Not that it appears to have affected his beliefs or behavior very much. When his friend Nancy Mitford asked him how he could be a Christian, given his character and inclinations, he assured her that if he weren't a Christian he would be "even more horrible."

I've heard that excuse before, and I don't buy it. Maybe Waugh did yearn for God and grace—but his writings suggest he was drawn to the church because he liked the antiquity of Catholicism, the tradition, and above all the exclusivity. The changes of the Second Vatican Council, especially the vernacular Mass, upset him. If he'd joined the church partially to claim membership in an elite society, imagine his distress when the doors were flung open, the walls brought down. It was supposed to be a special thing, just for him, like bananas in wartime—or like the fantasy world of aristocratic old England.

This temptation to elitism is a peril for Roman Catholics, myself included. One of the things that attracted me to Catholicism, in contrast with evangelical Protestantism, was that it seemed ritualistically exclusive and intellectually demanding. Since my university tended, in those days, toward a charismatic goofiness that was not to my taste, I avoided Mass at the chapel, and went to the more traditional liturgy downtown or drove with friends to a Latin Mass parish in the nearest big city. We were not about to let the accidents of geography prevent us from being *Brideshead Revisited* characters. Like Charles Ryder, I had been looking for magic, and I found it in my little circle of eccentrics, dressed up in flowy frocks and floppy hats, lounging under trees in the cemetery reading the poetry of Gerard Manley Hopkins and drinking cheap wine, savoring it like it was Château Peyraguey. I am still friends with two of the women from that long-ago circle. The others took very different paths, moving step by step away from our classical paradigm that, stodgy and naive though it was, had the merit of prizing free exchange of ideas, into a culture-war mentality marked with paranoia and a susceptibility to conspiracy theories.

Maybe it's less about Oxford, the stately home, and the French wine, and more about knowing in your bones that whatever you cling to is likely to pass away.

Forbidden desires

The wine and strawberries scene happens early in the novel, when Sebastian takes Charles to Brideshead for the first time. They recline in a grove of elms on a green knoll, smoking. "Just the place to bury a crock of gold," Sebastian says. "I should like to bury something precious in every place where I've been happy and then, when I was old and ugly and miserable, I could come back and dig it up and remember."[2] As a young reader I read and reread those lines, in melancholy anticipation for the nostalgia I too would feel, someday. What I didn't realize was that I would feel not just nostalgia, but regret.

SEBASTIAN KNOWS THAT HE will one day look back with hopeless nostalgia because he understands that his happiness is transient. His tragedy, hinted at in the narrative, is that he is gay. The official Catholic reading is that his homosexuality is his tragic flaw, his inability to align himself with traditional teaching the source of his unhappiness. Reading the novel

---

[2] Waugh, 24.

now, I see that the flaw is not in Sebastian, but in the world that condemns him. We Catholics joke about "Catholic guilt," but Sebastian's story is painfully like that of many LGBTQ+ young people, forced to hide their identity and suffering for it.

During my years as a teacher in conservative settings, I got to know many LGBTQ+ students, most of them delightful, thoughtful people. And almost all of them were closeted, due to the hostile environment they lived in. Professors and campus leaders regularly engaged in hate speech about LGBTQ+ people while claiming their expressions of condemnation and dehumanization were motivated by love. Maybe they really believed this, but the fruits of their actions were never positive. They caused pain and distress in a demographic already vulnerable. People who are LGBTQ+, according to the National Institute on Drug Abuse, have higher rates of, and more severe, substance use disorders than straight people do.[3] When LGBTQ+ people are subjected to suspicion, hostility, and discrimination, especially from those close to them, stress and isolation can intensify these disorders. Unfortunately, many Christians point to rates of depression, self-harm, and addiction in LGBTQ+ people and claim that their pain stems from sinful lifestyles. Yet when queer youth are accepted, welcomed, and allowed to be themselves, they have better lives and outcomes.

Sebastian never gets to be who he really is, outside the fantasy world he briefly creates for himself. Proximity to his

---

[3] National Institute on Drug Abuse, "LGBTQI+ People and Substance Use," May 2024.

family, and his family's expectations for him, remind him of the gap between who he is and who they demand he be. Of course he behaves vacuously, at times. And of course he drinks to excess. *Brideshead Revisited* is, in part, a gay love story with a tragic ending, but this is so subtly written that generations of conservative readers can wallow in the beauty and languor of the first chapters, without admitting they are swooning over a queer romance. Charles, by contrast, has no internalized guilt or shame over his erotic intimacy with his friend, so he drinks merrily without developing dependence. In his lack of guilt Charles is not unlike Waugh himself, who did not self-flagellate over his own youthful homosexual flings, which he considered (or claimed to consider) just a phase. Occasionally he expressed shame over his heavy drinking, and his frequent visits to his favorite sex worker, but he never overtly connected his bouts of depression with internalized homophobia.

For readers who miss the subtext, it's enough to say that Sebastian is an alcoholic. Even though this reading leaves out crucial aspects of the story, it is still painfully relatable to anyone who has loved a person with addiction and recognizes that destructive energy. Substance-use disorders may have their origins in or be exacerbated by stress and trauma, but they take on a life of their own. At a certain point the addiction simply is. Everything else is subsumed into it. And in *Brideshead Revisited,* addiction destroys Sebastian. Ultimately, he gets in trouble and has to leave college. The world he created with Charles is shattered, and he descends into addiction and self-destructive behavior. Charles helps him access alcohol because he's afraid Sebastian will shut him out completely if he doesn't. But Lady Marchmain, discovering what's going on, is enraged. Charles leaves Brideshead, sure he will never return.

But he does return. For a little while he remains connected with members of the family, and when Lady Marchmain becomes sick, Charles sets out to find Sebastian, to let him know that she'd like to see him one last time. Sebastian is in Morocco, weak and emaciated, convalescing from alcohol-related illness in a hospital run by Franciscans. He still radiates charm, however, even when conniving to get alcohol. A lay brother tells Charles about Sebastian's patience amid his suffering, and his kindness in taking in a starving German man he found on the streets. A "real Samaritan," the brother says, and Charles thinks, "poor simple monk, poor booby."

Charles's sneers at religion read like a caricature of an agnostic. Of course, the agnostic sneers at the good and wise friar. Of course he makes jokes trivializing sin. It's what agnostics do. But Charles's straw-man agnosticism seems set up deliberately to fail. Or maybe Charles really is that unoriginal. Either way, he's at his best when with Sebastian. Later, though he thrives socially and professionally, something is missing.

The second part of the novel feels like a desperate effort on Charles's part, and maybe on Waugh's as well, to recapture something lost forever. Lady Marchmain is dead. Sebastian is living in a monastery in Tunisia, though they won't let him be an actual monk, due to his alcoholism. Charles is a successful artist, with a career painting stately homes. On a ship returning from an art trip in the Americas, he meets Julia again. Both unhappy in their marriages, they begin an affair.

Waugh rarely makes a misstep in his prose, but some of his least inspired writing is in the Charles-and-Julia section of the story, even though, presumably, readers are meant to treat this as the more mature romance. Graham Greene, who was a friend of Waugh's, admired *Brideshead Revisited*, but was critical of some of the style, especially the description of Charles's first sexual encounter with Julia. "I took formal possession of her as her lover," Charles says. And, even worse, "I was made free of her narrow loins." It's not good writing, maybe partially because it reflects some of the banality of Charles and Julia's relationship. Charles may claim, following Waugh's own expressed theories, that his love for Sebastian was an adolescent preface to his more mature relationship with Julia, but it's the queer romance that feels more real, more profound.

This romance, by contrast, has its place in polite society, even if it is technically transgressive. But Julia is uncertain, distrustful of Charles. Things come to a head when her father, Lord Marchmain, comes home to his estate to die, and repents and returns to the church in his final moments. As a result of witnessing this, Julia breaks up with Charles. "Probably I shall be bad again, punished again," she says. "But the worse I am, the more I need God. I can't shut myself out from His mercy. That is what it would mean, starting a life with you, without Him." Staying with Charles, she says, would mean setting up a rival good to God's, the one unforgivable sin.

This feels like a stretch, as though Julia is plugging in some religious formula she learned somewhere. And it does not align with Catholic theology, anyway. There is no insurmountable Catholic rule saying that Charles and Julia can't divorce their spouses, have their loveless marriages annulled, and marry in the church. But Julia is in a vulnerable state. Her family is fractured, she's survived a bitter marriage, then along comes her wicked old father and his deathbed conversion. Maybe Julia is spooked. Maybe her conviction that she can't be with Charles is born out of a deep self-hatred, just as Sebastian drank because of self-hatred. Charles tells her that he understands. But a reader who hasn't been steeped in Catholic scrupulosity might not. We do find out, in the closing pages of *Brideshead Revisited,* that Charles eventually becomes Catholic as well—or is, at least, inclining toward Catholicism—when he steps into the old chapel in Brideshead and says a prayer, "an ancient, newly learned form of words."

The first time I taught *Brideshead Revisited,* I offered a conventional Catholic interpretation of the plot, in which Charles's youthful infatuation with Sebastian is a foretaste of the love he will later feel for Julia, which in turn is a foretaste of the love he will find in the church. "He was the forerunner," Charles says of Sebastian. And this makes Julia worry that she, too, is just a forerunner. Her worry is well founded. Waugh clearly intends Julia to be a stepping-stone toward God, just as Charles's youthful love for Sebastian was meant to be a stepping-stone to Julia (following Waugh's idiosyncratic ideas about gay versus straight relationships).

Revisiting Brideshead, physically and emotionally, is a chance for Charles to look back through the corridors of memory and understand that his heart was always restless because he was seeking God. In one scene, later in the book, Cordelia reminisces about her mother reading aloud from G. K. Chesterton's *The Wisdom of Father Brown*. The priest says of the thief that he caught him "with an unseen hook and an invisible line which is long enough to let him wander to the ends of the world and still to bring him back with a twitch upon the thread." God, as I said, has us all hooked and can draw us back to grace at any time.

The sanctity of queer love

This all looks beautiful as long as you stay inside the magic snow globe of Waugh's Catholicism. Step out, and you see things differently. This is a story about dysfunctional people who cling to religion because they need meaning and continuity in a fractured time, but the church basically destroys their lives.

But wait, you might object. Charles's life isn't ruined. He has God. And grace, mercy, and forgiveness.

That's the official, orthodox Catholic reading, but it's not really supported by the story itself. We can tell ourselves Charles has found God, and grace, but there's no evidence that anything substantially good, any justice or healing or liberation, has come from any of these characters' pain.

Step away from the obligation to believe that Charles must be better off because he is closer to the church, and you start to wonder if Charles missed his one chance for happiness forever—not with Julia, but with Sebastian, if traditional prohibitions on homosexuality hadn't come between them. Or maybe he could have been happy with Julia, if Catholic guilt hadn't compelled her to break things off. And the Catholic Church, which came between Charles and those he loved, now, ironically, is also the one thing connecting him to them, even tenuously, through the ritual of holy water, the liturgy in the same Latin, all the world over.

Or maybe he never could have been happy with either of them, and he's better off meeting them only in the chambers of memory, of which the church is the curator.

I find this interpretation more intriguing than the official Catholic one I told my students years ago. Maybe it's a fatalistic, pre-Christian sort of reading, but I don't see that as a problem because Waugh's vision of the world and humanity isn't especially Christian, anyway, if by Christian we mean anything connected with Jesus, the poor ragged Galilean and his radical teachings about healing and liberation. Waugh seems to want a pagan deity, a classical, transcendent God, who rides above it all—not a deity who enters history and stands with the oppressed. And the story he tells in *Brideshead Revisited* is of a man who is desperate to travel, not onward, but backward, to the time when he was happy, to the place where he buried the pot of gold.

I have found one way to read *Brideshead Revisited* from a Christian perspective that makes sense to me. But it requires us to set aside prejudice and consider the possibility that God was present for Charles from the start, not in some transcendent beyond, but in his love for Sebastian and Sebastian's love for him. If their love was tragic and doomed, this was because of the world they lived in. Sebastian didn't need to be tormented by his own conviction of guilt and unworthiness. He didn't need to be driven to alcoholic self-destruction. That was never what God wanted for him.

Evelyn Waugh unintentionally wrote a story that affirms the sanctity of queer love, the presence of the divine in Charles and Sebastian's connection with each other. Even with the destruction of Sebastian's life, he remains holy, and holds onto hope. Even with Charles's heartbreak, he has not given up on love and beauty. Revisiting Brideshead, and confronting the memories he has carried with him, does restore a flicker of hope. When Charles prays in the little chapel he first visited with Sebastian, he sees a red flame burning in the tabernacle. "It could not have been lit but for the builders and the tragedians, and there I found it this morning, burning anew among the old stones."[4]

The flame that he needed was here all along. Charles may not see it yet, but maybe readers of Waugh's novel can.

---

[4] Waugh, *Brideshead Revisited*, 351.

7

Graham Greene

A transgressive read

"O God, You've done enough, You've robbed me of enough, I'm too tired and old to learn to love, leave me alone for ever."

These lines, the close of Graham Greene's novel *The End of the Affair*, are my favorite last lines in English literature. At the start of the story the protagonist, Maurice Bendrix, states that "this is a record of hate far more than of love," and though he has burned through his hatred by the end of the story, he's hardly at peace. For some reason, I find this comforting. I like a novel that doesn't taunt me with cheery resolutions.

One of Greene's most overtly Catholic novels, *The End of the Affair* is frequently included on lists of modern Catholic classics. It was a popular book in my social circle, but I never read it for class, and we never discussed it at length, the way

we discussed *Brideshead Revisited*. Possibly we were too prud-
ish to be comfortable with Greene's directness about sex. Or
maybe we weren't sure what to do with a story in which the
protagonist does not, in the end, embrace God and grace. I
remember only one conversation I had about the book in my
university days. I was walking to school and an older graduate
student, married with small children, stopped to give me a
ride. He asked me what I was reading in my spare time, and I
said, "Graham Greene. *The End of the Affair.*" He nodded and
said, "I never really understood that book. I think I'd need to
have an affair to understand it."

I still don't know whether that was an inappropriate
flirtation, or just an awkward moment. But I wonder whether
we were reading Greene's novel because it was a surreptitious
way to be sexually transgressive. So much repression sim-
mered under the surface of our polite interactions, and we
were stupid about sex, relying on papal and ecclesial documents to define the moral parameters of the erotic. Multiple
people I knew, including one man I dated, were queer but in
denial. Many others (myself included) made bad marriages
and eventually divorced. It's sadly ironic that a subculture that
fixated on controlling sexual behavior was so clueless about
solid sexual ethics, or the practical realities of what makes a
healthy relationship.

And it wasn't just cluelessness. Publicly we assented to
conservative, patriarchal cultural mores around sex. Privately,
other things were happening. Unbeknownst to most of us,
one of the most popular priests on campus had developed a

pattern of sexually assaulting women students. Several of his fellow priests knew about it, and covered for him—including the university president, a man many regarded as a role model and even a saint. In graduate school, I had to deal with predatory behavior from several very conservative men who were very loud, in public, about the importance of traditional morals. And then there were the things I learned from my students, when I was teaching, about assault coverups and inappropriate behavior.

When the revelations came out, in early 2023, about how late theologian Jean Vanier not only used the communities he founded to sexually abuse women, but founded those communities precisely with that intent, I was reminded of the predatory priests at my college. Had some of those men sought out that school with the intent to prey on women? What kind of lies were they telling themselves? How much of the campus obsession with sexual morality, sexual purity, and modest dress was a cover for sexual obsession? Or an attempt to deflect guilt and shame?

The relationship in *The End of the Affair* is adulterous, and unhealthy, but it is consensual. Among ultra-conservative Catholics, the tendency is to lump together all sexual relationships that aren't married, heterosexual, and procreative, and treat them all as equally grave moral violations. Conservative political philosopher Russell Kirk, in his 1989 suspense novel *Lord of the Hollow Dark,* at one point has his hero imply that rapists are easier to reform than queer people, because at least rape is "natural." I've heard similar claims from several ultra-conservative Catholic academics. Understanding that their theory of sexual morality comes down to this simplistic dividing line can help explain why so many religiously conservative men argue that the contemporary world has rejected all sexual moral norms. They can't recognize that many in the secular world take values like consent, boundaries, mutuality, and safety seriously, because those values are not deemed morally relevant in their either/or framework.

So, no, we really weren't prepared to read Greene intelligently—whether he was writing about sex, or about God.

SET IN LONDON DURING the Blitz, *The End of the Affair* is the story of a cynical writer who, seeking material for a novel, befriends a civil servant and has an affair with his wife, Sarah. The two fall in love, but Maurice is a jealous, unhappy lover. One afternoon as they are together in Maurice's flat, a bomb hits the building, and he is knocked out. On regaining consciousness, he finds Sarah crouched naked near the bed. Seeing him alive she seems, not relieved, but upset. Immediately afterward, she breaks off their affair.

Assuming she's dumped him for a new lover, Maurice hires a private detective to spy on her. But what Maurice learns, when the detective steals Sarah's diary for him, is something unexpected: Sarah dumped him because of a bargain with God. After the bombing, Sarah, convinced Maurice was dead, threw herself on the ground and began to pray: Just let him be alive, and I'll give him up. She looked at him with horror when she realized he was alive, because she understood she had to keep her promise and end their affair. In her diary entries she agonizes, rages at God, and confesses her love for Maurice. But even as she rages, she is falling in love—not with a rival human lover, but with God.

Still convinced he can talk Sarah into coming back to him, Maurice goes to her house. She tries to get away from him, running out into the rain and entering a church. Maurice follows her in and begs her to leave Henry, but Sarah, who has been sick, says she is tired and will call him later. But Sarah does not call. A few days later Maurice learns from Henry that Sarah is dead.

The rest of the story focuses on Maurice's rage at God for taking Sarah from him. Each new detail that emerges—the fact that Sarah was planning to become Catholic, the revelation that she'd been baptized as a baby, stories of miraculous healings—feels like another blow. "You won in the end," he says to God. "I hate you. I hate you as though you existed." And then his prayer, the book's closing words, demanding that God leave him alone forever.

What happens next, we don't know. Maybe Maurice decides to be grateful for the love he had, or repent for the pain he caused. Maybe he moves on. He may even pull a Charles Ryder and follow his lost lover into the sanctum of the church. Greene doesn't tell us. Maybe he doesn't know. Endings are not always happy or redemptive or even very conclusive.

I appreciate Greene's honesty about this, and about the fact that divine entry into human life would be profoundly disruptive. The God who stands at the door and knocks is the annoying, unwelcome visitor. It would be theologically respectable to say that poor angry Maurice just needs to let go of corrupt human love and let God in. But I don't think that's Greene's point.

As novelists, Waugh and Greene are often classed together. Like Waugh, Greene was a convert to Catholicism but not a noticeable moral person. His novels are taken seriously by the secular literary world. Greene, like Waugh, adds spiritual intrigue to the traditional adultery novel by bringing God into it. But unlike Waugh, he does it convincingly. While Sebastian, Julia, and Charles torment themselves over abstractions, there's nothing abstract about the power that shatters Maurice's affair with Sarah. Something real entered into their lives. But Greene's relationship with his own faith was ambiguous, as was the role of religion in his stories, so we should be cautious about tacking triumphalist interpretations onto them.

The Christian agnostic

Greene was born in 1904 in Hertfordshire, a county near London. As a boy he was inclined to melancholy and depression, and an unhappy school experience exacerbated this to the point that he made several suicide attempts. Because of Greene's self-mythologizing, it's difficult to ascertain from his autobiography whether he truly intended self-harm. According to his brother, he played Russian roulette—but with an unloaded revolver. Later, he would self-medicate for depression by drinking heavily and taking opium.

Greene went on to study history at Balliol College, Oxford, where he kept largely to himself. Waugh, who was at Oxford at the same time, described Greene as aloof and antisocial. During his time at Oxford, Greene met the writer Vivien Dayrell-Browning, who was Catholic. The two fell in love, but she refused to marry him unless he was baptized into her church. One could flippantly call this a conversion of convenience, but that wouldn't do justice to the seriousness with which Greene thought about God, religion, morality, and ultimate things, despite the chasm that existed between traditional Catholic ethics and his lifestyle. In his middle years, he stopped receiving the Catholic sacraments, but resumed them again near the end of his life.

Greene's marriage to Dayrell-Browning was probably doomed from the start. He was volatile, easily bored, and plagued by the same mental-health issues that had troubled him in his teens, which were eventually diagnosed as manic depression (known today as bipolar disorder). And then there were the affairs. Greene took sexual promiscuity to the level of obsession, frequently seeking out sex workers and having both serious affairs and passing flings. He especially enjoyed having sexual encounters in public or semi-public places, including on trains and (supposedly) behind church altars.

He and Vivien had two children, but Greene was never close to them. During World War II, Vivien and the children went to the country to shelter from the air raids. In their absence Greene stayed with his lover Dorothy Glover, which saved his life when the Greenes' home was bombed. Though this episode inspired *The End of the Affair,* the character of Sarah was inspired not by Glover, but by Catherine Walston, with whom Greene became obsessed shortly after. In 1947, Greene and Dayrell-Browning separated, but never divorced, due to her Catholic convictions. Dayrell-Browning would later become a world-renowned expert in the history of doll houses.

Greene published his first novel in 1929, while carrying on his work as a journalist, and went on to write twenty-four novels, both thrillers and more serious works—though even when crafted for a popular audience, his stories, which explore suffering, doubt, temptation, and questions about good and evil, are far from lighthearted. He also wrote essays, poetry, and two autobiographies. To seek material for his writing he traveled widely, often to places known for danger or civil unrest. Over the course of his career he traveled in Liberia, Mexico, Haiti, the Congo, Cuba, Vietnam, and Argentina. In 1941, the British foreign intelligence service MI6 recruited him as a spy—work that would inspire a number of his literary works. He also spent time in pre-revolutionary Cuba, then seedy and corrupt. Despite his cynicism, Greene sympathized with the revolutionaries. He was acquainted with Fidel Castro, and even aided the rebels by transporting clothing for them.

Greene eventually retired to Vivey, a town in Switzerland near Lake Leman. In 1986, he was awarded Britain's Order of Merit. Five years later, at the age of eighty-six, he died of leukemia.

ROBERT ROYAL, IN A 1999 article for *First Things*, writes that "Greene's character flaws and Cold War fantasies led to the extinction of a great gift. He went from being the premier English novelist of the soul to an enabler of later and lesser lights who let their appetites and resentments rule their talents."[1] This is a far-fetched claim: Greene's gift was never extinguished. If anything, his skepticism made his writing more powerful. But at least Royal sees the difficulty of trying to enlist Greene in the culture war. In his day, Greene was eyed with suspicion by the Vatican, and I expect that the conservative Catholics who admire his writing today would have disavowed him while he was alive.

Greene would probably be fine with this. He referred to himself as a "Catholic agnostic," and didn't like being called a Catholic writer. Once he wrote to Catherine Walston that he got more out of going to Mass when she was around. "I'm a much better Catholic in mortal sin!" he told her. In both his life and his work, Greene tested the limits of faith against his own capacity to violate it. Ben Granger, in an article for *Spike Magazine*, writes:

> There must be a suspicion Greene was playing with the Faith for his own sense of internal drama, much like Dali, whose use of the religion was a prop to adorn his art with ever more outlandishly theological accoutrements. Catholicism is after all,

---

[1] Robert Royal, "The (Mis)guided Dream of Graham Greene," *First Things*, November 1999.

a religion of the picturesquely ornate, of the dra-
matic. The stained glass and incense filled churches, the arcane blood and flesh fuelled doctrines of
transubstantiation, the unflinchingly Manichean
morality, the sheer ancient grim majesty of it all.
This is truly the religion of the drama queen.[2]

Granger notes, too, that Greene was "a poor advertisement
for the familiar argument of religion being a solace in life,
the 'heart in a heartless world.'" His stories, like Dostoevsky's,
depict encounters with the divine that occur outside the
boundaries of respectability, to those who have violated societal codes, or reached the end of their endurance. But when
God shows up, it's not comforting. In a world full of problems
and uncertainty, God becomes the biggest problem of all.

I'VE THOUGHT A LOT about the misery of Sarah's answered
prayer in *The End of the Affair*. Religious people like to talk
eloquently about the "intrusion" of God into ordinary human
life, but do we think about just how intrusive it would really
be, if God were to show up? How a miracle could throw
everything off-kilter?

Back in my hyper-religious undergraduate days, everyone was alert for signs and wonders, and usually managed
to find them. Everyone's rosaries were always turning gold
(it was just paint rubbing off). People faked speaking in

---

[2] Ben Granger, "The Literary and Political Catholicism of Graham
Greene and Evelyn Waugh," *Spike Magazine*, May 19, 2008.

tongues, faked being "slain in the spirit." The more extreme our piety, the better our social standing. Sometimes we talked about how we'd welcome martyrdom, and fantasized about an imaginary secular regime that would persecute us for our faith. For a little while, I prayed to have an apparition of Mary, like the three Fatima children, Lucia, Jacinta, and Francisco. Now, reading about these children makes me sad. Before they became famous visionaries, they lived normal lives. Afterward, they lived in terror of hell, inflicting mortifications on themselves. Jacinta and Francisco died young. Lucia went into a convent and was harassed by conspiracy theorists all her life. We fetishized the suffering of dead children while ignoring the injustice done to real living children in our world.

For a few months, my parents lived on a commune where an ex-convict claimed to be having apparitions of Mary. When people gathered to pray the rosary, they always saw crosses in the sky (they were airplane contrails). By then I had already grown skeptical of the frenzy of devotion, but doubting the people around me was not the same as doubting God or the church or miracles.

Now, when I consider the lives of the saints, I can't realistically say I want any of what they experienced. "Lord, if this is how you treat your friends, no wonder you have so few of them," St. Teresa of Avila is supposed to have said to God. Christians sometimes quote this glibly. But Greene's stories invite us to interrogate that glibness. St. Teresa may have made a joke of it, but her question arose out of deep and genuine pain. Why have we developed a religious imagination that glosses over this? And why do we think God wants us to suffer, anyway? As though our only way to God is through martyrdom, not through ordinary everyday happiness, even ordinary corrupt human love?

Living with ambiguities

In his 1938 crime thriller *Brighton Rock*, Greene tests an article of faith dear to progressive Christians: the belief that everyone, deep down, is basically good. *Brighton Rock* is the story of Pinkie, a teenage criminal sociopathic who cold-bloodedly woos and marries a waitress, Rose, to prevent her from testifying against him in a trial. Like Vladimir Nabokov's *Lolita* and Umberto Eco's *The Prague Cemetery, Brighton Rock* puts the reader inside the psyche of a deeply disturbed and disturbing individual.

Pinkie and Rose are both Catholic, but it's the only thing they have in common. For Pinkie, who comes from society's dregs, Catholicism's categories of good and evil allow him to assert power. In choosing evil, he claims existential mastery. Disgusted by Rose's sentimentality, he relishes the idea that his evil triumphs over her goodness: "She was good, but he'd got her like you got God in the Eucharist—in the guts. God couldn't escape the evil mouth which chose to eat its own damnation."[3] When we talk about God manifest

---

[3] Graham Greene, *Brighton Rock* (New York: Bantam Books, 1968), 177.

in human flesh, made vulnerable in the incarnation, do we think about how a God made vulnerable is also a God made violable? Pinky does.

Even knowing that Pinkie is a criminal, Rose adores him, and thinks he adores her in return. It's the classic "I can save him" thing. On their wedding night, at her suggestion, they record messages for one another on a gramophone, to listen to later. But when Rose leaves Pinkie alone to record his secret message, he says what he is really thinking: "God damn you, you little bitch, why can't you go back home for ever and let me be?"[4]

Later, Pinkie convinces Rose to make a suicide pact, hoping she'll die first so he can be rid of her, but the plan goes awry, and he's the one who ends up dead. Rose, distraught over the idea that her beloved is in hell, talks to a priest, who reassures her: "You can't conceive, my child, nor can I, or anyone—the . . . appalling . . . strangeness of the mercy of God."[5] And Rose is relieved. She holds onto the idea of Pinkie's love for her, believing it can redeem him. Then she remembers the recording he made. She can hear his voice again! The book ends with Rose walking, at peace, back to her house, back to the final horror that awaits her. No happy endings here. Not even a dip into a holy water stoup.

Brighton Rock undermines a popular theme in great Christian literature, the idea that everyone is salvageable, and that grace can show up even in our lowest moments.

---

[4] Greene, 176.
[5] Greene, 247.

There is no grace for Pinkie. He's not a Dostoevsky character encountering Christ in his own sin and wretchedness. And it certainly seems like his hate, in the end, is more powerful than Rose's love. So much for "love conquers all."

Pinkie may be fictional, but moral monsters are real, and history is full of them: the mass murderers, serial killers, agents of genocide. Are they beyond God's redeeming power? Greene does not leave us with an answer.

IN 1940, TWO YEARS after *Brighton Rock*, Greene published *The Power and the Glory*, which also deals with sin and redemption. On the surface, the plot is simple. It's Mexico in the 1930s, and in the anti-Catholic state of Tabasco a priest, whose name we never learn, is on the run from the police. The priest never set out to be a reformer or radical. Prior to the state's persecution of Catholics, he was an ordinary parish priest, a complacent man who took pleasure in the admiration of parishioners and the soft ease of clerical life. Now, reduced to poverty and fleeing from the law, he has not become pure or holy. He has become an alcoholic. Greene calls him a "whisky priest."

In a moment of drunkenness and despair, the whisky priest fathered a child with a peasant woman. The child is ugly, malicious, with an unsettling adult awareness. Though the priest, returning to his village, is appalled by the child's malice, he also feels a deep love for her and a desire for her salvation. This is the conundrum of divine charity, that God loves us, even at our worst. But if the ugly, malicious child is like humanity, does that mean that God is like the whisky priest? Flawed, often useless, but willing to die for us, even though it does no discernible good?

DESPITE HIS MANY FAILURES, the priest carries on, one step ahead of the police, doggedly caring for his flock, while berating himself for his sins, and wondering what the point is. He hears furtive confessions, says rapid Masses, then moves on. Some people aid him. Others want nothing to do with him. One man, who latches onto him for a time, ultimately betrays him. The motif of martyrdom is highlighted by vignettes depicting a pious woman in one of the villages, reading to her children from the lives of Native martyrs. Her daughters listen dutifully but their brother is scornful of the saccharine, interested only in the elements of violence or heroism. The priest is pursued by a ruthless lieutenant who, like Javert in *Les Miserables*, is obsessed with finding his prey. In his eagerness to eradicate the last representative of an unjust church, he violates his own principles of justice, taking hostages from every village the priest has visited, and shooting them if they refuse to confess where he is. When the Judas character betrays the priest, the lieutenant captures him, and the two discover in conversation that they grudgingly admire each other. The lieutenant even tries to help the priest find a confessor, but it doesn't work out, and the priest is shot and dies unshriven. The lieutenant is convinced he has murdered the last priest, and the pious woman adds him to her litany of saints and martyrs.

In the final scene of the novel, a stranger appears in town. He knocks at the door of the pious woman and her son opens the door. "I am a priest," the stranger says. The boy puts his finger to his lips and welcomes him in. Here, at last, is the heroism he was looking for.

WE CAN READ *THE Power and the Glory* as highlighting the resilience of faith in times of suffering, but only if we ignore the story's ambiguities. The priest and the lieutenant are not only adversaries but doubles, both fanatically dedicated to their beliefs while simultaneously violating them. Each sees in the other his arch-nemesis and his own reflection. And both are right, too. The church has been a comforter, as the priest believes. The church has also been an oppressor, as the lieutenant believes. So what's the truth? Maybe somewhere out of reach. Near the end of the story, when the priest briefly believes he is safe, he senses the return of his old complacent piety and realizes that this, not his drinking or cowardice or lust, is what has made him a bad priest all along. When he loses his certainty, he grows closer to God. And that faith, though fragile and imperfect, feels real.

The faith of the *Brideshead Revisited* people, by contrast, seems artificial. Their choices can all be explained without having to bring God into the story, or without God being a real person. Charles's prayer, at the end, seems like something Waugh made him do. Whereas Sarah Miles, stopping to dip her finger in the "so-called holy water," as she leaves the church in a "flaming rage," feels like something a real person would do. At any rate, I could imagine myself doing it.

A few years ago, in London, I had a chance to visit that church. Despite my deep disillusionment with the institutional church and its role in US politics, I felt I could pray there—in the company of make-believe characters invented by a dead man who had been a drug addict and a sex fiend and who ditched the church for much of his life. In that space between reality and unreality, I was aware that I had not completely lost my religious sense, my desire for meaning and connection, my hope that all will somehow be made right.

WHEN IT COMES TO Greene's work, I realize, what I needed to deconstruct was not his writing, but the mythos that has been created around it, a culture of reading that deliberately skirts the difficult questions and reinterprets his religious themes to make them more comfortable. Greene himself holds up, post-deconstruction. If anything, he makes more sense to me now. I may even understand, a bit, what the whisky priest experienced, when he realized that the church was making him bad. The priest sticks with the church, for all that, but Greene doesn't force us to put a comforting interpretation on this. He allows us to sit with our contradictions and uncertainties. And I trust him, the perpetually unfaithful Graham Greene, because he isn't lying to me. He is honest about how hard it is to make sense of suffering, in a world that doesn't always match up with our dogmas and creeds.

8

C. S. Lewis

Getting beyond the binary

I used to be a gender essentialist. I believed all human beings could be sorted into one of two fixed gender categories, each determined by an unalterable essence revealing itself through distinct characteristics. This ideology was so fundamental to my conservative outlook, it stayed with me for years, even through my studies of feminist philosophy and gender theory. Not until I started teaching a class on philosophy of the person did I decide to double check my assumptions against natural science, to see whether the real world matched my theories.

Having spent years on a ranch, I already knew that nature is more complicated than conservative theorists imagine. But just a little reading about sexuality and reproduction in different species made me aware that our categories of male and female, useful as they are for taxonomy, only work if we allow for gray areas and gradations. Not only do some animals engage in same-sex mating behavior, but gendered roles and behaviors in the animal kingdom are incredibly diverse and varied. In many species, females are bigger and more aggressive than males. Sometimes the females eat the males. The female seahorse deposits her eggs into a pouch under the male's tail. Then the male fertilizes the eggs, incubates the embryos, and gives birth. Gender isn't fixed, either. Multiple species, including some fish, birds, and amphibians can change their sex. Some species, including snails, earthworms, clownfish, starfish, and some shrimp, are hermaphroditic. And many varieties of intersex conditions exist, in both human and nonhuman animals.

The more I read, the more I realized gender essentialism was an inadequate framework for the vast diversity of the real world. So I decided to stop being a gender essentialist. Even after all those years of conservatism, I found it surprisingly easy to shrug off that old ideology—thanks to, of all people, C. S. Lewis.

OFTEN REGARDED AS THE most influential Christian apologist of the twentieth century, Lewis is beloved of conservative Christians, and many of his views on gender, as expressed in his fiction, are pretty traditionalist. There's that scene in *The Lion, the Witch, and the Wardrobe* where Father Christmas tells Susan and Lucy that they won't be joining the fight against the White Witch, because "battles are ugly when women fight." Then there's the "evil witch" trope in the Narnia books, the sexist fear of powerful, disobedient, seductive women tempting the poor hapless males out of their virtuous path. And, of course, there's the ending Lewis gives to Susan Pevensie, who gets left out of paradise on account of the unspeakable sin of caring about "nylons and lipstick and invitations." Even though Lewis stated later that Susan's story isn't over and she still has hope of being saved, this hardly helps. Why would her salvation be at risk, simply because she likes lipstick and boys? Maybe the idea is that superficiality is the unforgivable sin, but Lewis doesn't find it problematic for young men to be interested in sports or outdoor activities. Only feminine-coded frivolities endanger the soul.

While gender isn't a major theme in Narnia, it is a top concern in Lewis's *Space Trilogy*, especially the third book, *That Hideous Strength*, in which the hero, Elwin Ransom, doles out all kinds of ludicrous advice about marriage, sex, and gender. Ransom has never been married himself, and has probably never been sexually active, but the heavenly beings he chats with give him all the information he needs about sexual relationships. (Catholics who have been given terrible marriage advice by celibate priests may find this detail amusing.) At one point in the novel, Ransom counsels a young woman whose husband treats her dismissively and tells her it's her own fault since she had the gall to put off having children for the sake of her career, and because she "never attempted obedience." When she complains that her husband doesn't treat her as an equal, Ransom is appalled. There's no equality in marriage, he informs her. The subtext is that this is meant to be erotic knowledge: women who want to be sexually satisfied in marriage must submit to their husbands.

Lewis also hammers home the heteronormativity and homophobia with his representation of a psychopathic lesbian cop who enjoys torturing women, and a sinister Italian eunuch who abhors the idea of reproduction. Not surprisingly, both these characters are described as physically grotesque.

Despite all this, I still credit *That Hideous Strength* for getting me thinking beyond the binary. Lewis was a complicated man, who mixed intriguing ideas with tedious ones. He was a person who changed over time.

A Christian humanist

Originally from Ireland, Clive Staples Lewis was known to his friends, for much of his life, as Jack (a name he chose for himself as a child, in honor of a beloved pet dog). Lewis's mother died when he was nine, and his father sent him to England for school. He found the British education system depressing and sadistic. Between the unpleasantness of his school experiences and the loss of his mother, he had difficulty believing in an all-good and all-powerful creator and became an atheist while in his teens. He also became fascinated with Irish, Norse, and Greek mythology, and with the occult.

Shortly after starting at University College, Oxford, Lewis was sent to fight in France. Before the age of twenty he experienced the horrors of trench warfare and was wounded in action. After returning to Oxford, he studied classics, philosophy, and English, then went on to work as a fellow in English literature at Magdalen College, a post he held until 1954.

Based on Lewis's opinions in *That Hideous Strength,* one might picture him as priggish and judgmental, but he defies easy categorization. Despite his dehumanizing representations of sexual minorities, his views on homosexuality were less intolerant than one would expect. In *Surprised by Joy: The Shape of My Early Life,* he writes with some sympathy about adolescent gay relationships in British public schools, suggesting that they offered a rare glimmer of happiness even in a dismal cutthroat world. *His approach to sex and romance was hardly traditional, either.* While in the army, he and a friend, Edward Moore, made a pact. If either died, the survivor would care for the other's family. Moore was killed, so Lewis moved in with Moore's mother, Janie, who was thirty years his senior. Likely there were attachment issues at play: Lewis was motherless, and his father was distant. But some close to them suspected they were lovers. Lewis and Moore, along with his brother and her daughter, lived together for years, until she succumbed to dementia and went into a nursing home, where Lewis visited her daily until her death in 1951.

A year earlier, Lewis had begun a correspondence with American poet and scholar Joy Davidman, who was married at the time to writer William Lindsay Gresham, the author of *Nightmare Alley.* Davidman came from a secular Jewish family. She was a child prodigy, an atheist, and a member of the Communist Party. Her marriage to Gresham, an abusive alcoholic, was miserable, but for a time the two turned to Christianity as a possible cure for their marital woes. While their newfound faith couldn't save their marriage, it did bring Davidman closer to Lewis, who by then had an international reputation as a popular theologian. After her marriage finally disintegrated, she moved to England, where Lewis helped her and her sons financially.

Davidman was attracted to Lewis, but he initially felt only friendship and esteem for her. When her visa expired, he offered to marry her so she could stay in England, and she agreed. At first, they lived separately, until Davidman learned she had terminal cancer. That's when Lewis realized he had fallen in love with her. The two had a Christian marriage and were able to enjoy two somewhat normal years together while Davidman's cancer was in remission. But the disease returned, and she died in 1960. Grief-stricken, Lewis struggled to maintain his faith and began to suffer from health ailments. He died only three years after Davidman, at age sixty-four.

Though Lewis is celebrated among Christians for his apologetics and his speculative fiction, he was a widely published scholar, especially in the fields of medieval and Renaissance literature. His informal literary circle, known as the Inklings, comprised writers and academics who were interested in mythology, narrative fiction, and fantasy writing. Though they were not an explicitly Christian group, it was partially through his friendship with some of the Inklings, especially

J. R. R. Tolkien, that Lewis returned to Christianity, in 1931. He was also influenced by the works of George MacDonald, a Scottish minister and fantasy writer of the Victorian era, whom Lewis regarded as a master.

Lewis was less interested in interdenominational disputes than in the basics of the Christian creed. This may have been one reason why, despite Tolkien's urging, he never converted to Catholicism. In both his apologetics and his fiction, Lewis focuses on broad questions about creation, redemption, wrongdoing, humanity's relation to the universe, and the afterlife. This makes his writings unusually accessible not only to Christians from a wide range of backgrounds, but to non-Christians as well. Ultimately, he was no reactionary, but a Christian humanist, with a curious, questioning mind. Throughout his life he befriended diverse people of varying beliefs, seeking friendships with those he found intelligent and interesting, even when their views were very different from his.

In loving a woman who was brilliant, independent, and bold, Lewis changed some of his views on women, sex, gender, and marriage. In later books in the *Narnia* series, he revised his stance on women fighting. In *The Horse and His Boy*, Lucy, now a queen, joins in battle as an archer, and in *The Last Battle*, Jill fights bravely alongside the men. And in his final work of fiction, *Till We Have Faces*, a novel based on the myth of Eros and Psyche, Lewis made a complete turnaround. His protagonist, Orual, is a powerful queen. She's ugly, passionate, cunning, just, and a fierce fighter. And Lewis partially based her character on Davidman.

Lewis versus the technocratic paradigm

Lewis wrote the *Space Trilogy* (sometimes called the *Cosmic Trilogy* or the *Ransom Trilogy*) between 1938 and 1945. *Out of the Silent Planet* introduces the character of Elwin Ransom, a philologist who is kidnapped and taken in a spacecraft to the planet Mars, called Malacandra by its inhabitants. One of his captors is a flashy money-man named Devine, who hopes to mine for gold on Mars so he can get rich, buy a yacht, and surround himself with beautiful women. The other is a megalomaniacal scientist who believes any action is justified in order to achieve his end of human interplanetary domination. When they arrive on Mars, Ransom escapes and uses his philological skills to communicate with the Malacandrians, a group comprised of three separate but harmonious species.

Lewis depicts a natural world full of diversity, flashes of color, multiple species living side by side. One of the Malacandrians, in conversation with Ransom, remarks that having only one rational species on Earth must have "far reaching effects in the narrowing of sympathies and even of thought."[1] In Narnia, too, there is harmony in difference, beings from different mythologies and cultural traditions coexisting: talking animals, Roman fauns, Father Christmas, fairy-tale witches, Germanic dwarves. And this colorful diversity is a good thing. Having everyone act alike is usually, in Lewis's world, a bad sign. In *The Silver Chair*, for instance, the Green Witch

---

[1] C. S. Lewis, *Out of the Silent Planet* (New York: Scribner, 1938), 102.

enchants her subjects to think, act, and talk the same. At the end of *The Last Battle*, the dwarfs who become xenophobes ("The Dwarfs for the Dwarfs!") remain locked within their own minds, unable to see even the possibility of paradise. Christian commenters have pointed to this scene as an indictment of unbelief, and maybe that's what Lewis intended, but notable is how with unbelief comes xenophobia, a refusal to reach across dividing lines. Unity amid diversity is good. The desire to assert dominance and wipe out difference is evil.

The *Space Trilogy* invites readers to take a God's-eye view of these destructive human inclinations we so easily assume to be natural. In *Out of the Silent Planet*, in addition to the organic beings native to the place, there are immaterial intelligences called *eldila*, of whom the Oyarsa are the most powerful. From him, Ransom learns the terrible truth about his home planet: Earth is a kind of cosmic no-man's land, off limits to the other rational beings of the universe, and ruled by a rebel Oyarsa that has turned evil. The free *eldila*, who regularly visit other planets, are unable to visit there. This is why the Malacandrians call Earth the silent planet. No message goes in or out. Humanity's violence and xenophobia relate to the evil brought upon it by its spiritual ruler (obviously, Lewis intends us to understand Earth's rebel Oyarsa to be Satan).

In the second book, *Perelandra*, which is probably the most explicitly Christian in the trilogy, Ransom travels into space once again, this time as an interplanetary emissary. The Oyéresu send him to prevent Earth's ruler from spreading evil to the new inhabitants of the planet Venus. Weston, the sinister scientist from the first novel, arrives on Venus possessed by Earth's fallen Oyarsa and tries to tempt the "Eve" of that new creation into sin and disobedience. Ransom's task is to prevent this. In the end, he has to physically fight the possessed scientist, and though he is wounded, he triumphs. Perelandra is safe, and Ransom is returned to Earth.

I find *Perelandra* the least engaging of the Space Trilogy novels, partially because it feels too aggressively allegorical. Yet it can't be reduced to mere speculative fiction for Christians, or religious propaganda. Despite the overtly Christian ideas in most of his fiction, Lewis isn't just retelling the Christian story. He is trying to tell the human story, asking ultimate questions about our place in the universe and exploring Christianity's attempts to answer these questions. What if beings with intellect and will exist in other worlds? If original sin is real, how might it affect other species? If God decided to become present in other worlds, what would this be like? And how might other mythologies intersect with the Christian mythos?

So, in *That Hideous Strength*, which connects modern space travel to the ancient lore of Britain, Lewis tries to make sense of twentieth-century evils by relating them to legends of King Arthur, envisioning the moral struggles of his day as part of an ongoing cosmic drama. Unlike the first two books, this one takes place on Earth. The protagonists are a young married couple, Jane and Mark Studdock, both academics. Mark has recently become a senior fellow at his college and finally achieved his ambition of being part of the inner circle of the school's progressive element, which is trying to bring a new institute to his college (the National Institute for Coordinated Experiments, referred to by the acronym N.I.C.E.). Lewis depicts the college progressives as almost cartoonishly gauche and humorless, in keeping with his general distrust of the concept of progress, which I first encountered in the *Narnia* books, especially *The Voyage of the Dawn Treader*, where Eustace's awful family and experimental school are presented as progressive, and Prince Caspian says, of progress and development, "We call it *going bad*, in Narnia."

In my conservative days I sometimes referenced these quotations to attack liberal, progressive ideologies. But using Lewis in this way is anachronistic. Progressivism in Lewis's day was not 2020s progressivism. It involved some worthy causes, such as labor reform and women's rights, but also eugenics and medical experimentation. So Lewis's critiques are usually directed at ideologies not only repudiated by today's progressives, but advanced by right-leaning technocrats. Lewis-style villains are to be found among fascist-adjacent tech bros, or billionaire moguls who dream of exploiting nature and colonizing other worlds, weeding out "undesirables," and further enriching the "natural masters." Lewis is wary, too, of the idea that human culture automatically trends in a good direction, a distrust that is merited, and echoed in ideas about how we need to work together to bend the arc of history toward justice because left to its own devices it's unlikely to get there.

The most extreme example of the technocratic "progress" Lewis critiques is, of course, the Nazi regime. But it wasn't just the Nazis. In 1927, in the United States, the Supreme Court ruling *Buck v. Bell* decreed that inmates of mental institutions could be sterilized, a ruling that actually inspired Germany's project of forced sterilization. Then there was the infamous Tuskegee Syphilis Study: Between 1932 and 1972 the US Public Health Service recruited several hundred low-income Black men to be subjects of a study on untreated syphilis, without getting their consent or disclosing the details of the study, and without offering them treatment even when it became available. Yet this was all in the name of progress.

Lewis's "progressive" villains are anything but champions of social justice. Their comments about low-income laborers and retirees sound eerily familiar in the present US cultural scene, as does their yearning to cut the "red tape" of government restrictions on science or corporations, so they can get down to business. And the business they want to get down to is unrelievedly awful. Nevertheless, in *That Hideous Strength*, Mark Studdock is desperate to get in with them. What he doesn't realize at first is that N.I.C.E is not just focused on eliminating "undesirable" elements and creating gentrified communities. Their interest in his college is due to a legend that the body of the Arthurian character Merlin is buried on an ancient section of college property, not dead but sleeping. The plan is to resurrect Merlin and, using the combination of ancient magic and modern technology, replace humanity with a technocratic master race.

Meanwhile Mark's wife, Jane, finds her way into the heart of an unlikely resistance led by none other than Ransom, now known as the Pendragon, the living successor to King Arthur. They know Merlin really is sleeping under the grounds of the college, and know the N.I.C.E gang intends to reanimate him. The plot twist is that Merlin, once awakened, turns out to be on their side. The heavenly beings known as the Oyéresu have awakened him in order to use him in the fight against evil.

An unlikely gender theorist

This is where Lewis's gender theory comes in. As the Oyéresu descend to Earth through Merlin, we learn that each of them corresponds to one of the planets, and to the equivalent classical god (Mercury, Venus, etc.). And the Oyéresu, though not organic beings, have genders. The rulers of Mars and Mercury are masculine, and the ruler of Venus is feminine. So far, this looks like plain old Platonic essentialism. But surprise! These are not the only genders. Lewis imagines Mercury, Venus, and Mars as representing "those two of the Seven Genders that bear a certain analogy to the biological sexes."[2] Nor is there a perfect, fixed overlap between sex and gender: men can be feminine, too, in relation to their creator. Ransom tells Jane that "what is above and beyond all things is so masculine that we are all feminine in relation to it."[3]

---

[2] C. S. Lewis, *That Hideous Strength* (New York: Scribner, 1945), 322.
[3] Lewis, 313.

Lewis's cosmic gender theory is not always consistent; he implies that there are other, older, more powerful genders, so why default to treating God as masculine? Why make masculinity a superior gender at all? Some of this is just old-fashioned sexism, but Lewis is also playing around with some intriguing ideas that allow him to break out, in places, from the confines of patriarchal essentialism. *That Hideous Strength,* despite its reactionary notions about marriage, gender roles, and sexuality, offers the reader permission to question. When I first read the novel I was still ultra-conservative, yet I found Lewis's ideas about multiple genders attractive. I'd always felt constrained by essentialist expectations surrounding the feminine, so the possibility that there was more to gender identity was appealing, and it stuck with me, even though I officially ascribed to essentialism and complementarianism. Over the years, thanks to Lewis, I played with different approaches to the concept of gender. Maybe there weren't just two. Maybe gender wasn't fixed. Maybe it was relational, maybe something more like an aesthetic, versus a set of rigid categories rooted in sexual characteristics.

Some critics of *The Space Trilogy,* including the neo-Darwinist scientist J. B. S. Haldane, saw the book as anti-science, since Lewis portrayed so many scientists as villains. It's a criticism that should be taken seriously, especially considering contemporary trends of anti-science in some Christian subcultures. Yet I don't think Lewis was anti-science in the way of an anti-vaxxer or geocentrist. His distrust of scientists may have been a reaction, in part, to the Nazi atrocities of his time. But it was also connected with his resistance to rigidity; despite treating certain conventions as essential norms, Lewis thought it was a mistake to treat natural processes as universal laws. As the character Doctor Grace Ironwood says: "The laws of the universe are never broken. Your mistake is to think that the little regularities we have observed on one planet for a few hundred years are the real unbreakable laws; whereas they are only the remote results which the true laws bring about more often than not; as a kind of accident." Another character, Arthur Denniston, agrees: "And that is why nothing in Nature is quite regular. There are always exceptions. A good average uniformity, but not complete."[4] This happens to be a pretty good description of how our gender categories work. They may be useful for general categorization, but they don't give a complete picture.

After reading *The Chronicles of Narnia* as a child, I started going through the house opening closets, hoping one might lead to a different, magical realm. And I never quite stopped looking for that enchanted door. Maybe I'll never find one that leads to Narnia, but I've found other portals, enchanted gates, magical passages, out of intellectual confinement into the wide world of reality. So maybe it's not so weird after all that the creator of Narnia is also the writer who first offered me a pathway out of gender essentialism.

I get that readers who have deconstructed might prefer theological speculative fiction that isn't tainted by sexism and

---

[4] Lewis, 366.

queerphobia (and we haven't even touched on the Islamo-
phobia in the Narnia books), so I'm not going to judge those
who dislike Lewis's work. But those of us who still enjoy his
writing shouldn't feel we have to give up that enjoyment.
There's more to Lewis than his bigoted ideas, and his own
moral evolution demonstrates that people can learn and
change—just as we have.

9

J. R. R. Tolkien

A wizard among us

In 2021, a virtual seminar entitled "Tolkien and Diversity," organized by the Tolkien Society, prompted a racist, homophobic backlash. A year later, far-right trolls, angry about the diverse casting on *The Rings of Power,* review-bombed it so badly that Amazon suspended user ratings. This was depressing, but not surprising. For years, conservatives have viewed Middle-earth as their own private territory. Among traditionalist Catholics, Tolkien is frequently paired with Chesterton as patron of a quaint masculine subculture where misogyny and racism lurk beneath the pipe smoke.

But it was not always so. When I first discovered *The Lord of the Rings,* mine was a niche fandom, a little past its prime, associated with 1960s counterculturalism—even if not everyone flaunting a "Frodo Lives" button had read the books. In the 1980s, being a fantasy nerd was not cool. And this was during the "Satanic panic," when Christians eyed anything associated with wizards or magic as gateways to the occult. Expressing love for fantasy was something you did at your own risk. It was a risk I took. I'd been obsessed with Middle-earth since I was seven and caught the tail end of the 1978 animated film on TV. My mother then directed me to the volumes. I still remember the thrill I felt, pulling those three fat books from their slipcase: the 1973 edition, with watercolor paintings by the author on the covers.

I fell in love with Tolkien's world immediately. After trying to find a door to Narnia, I was now looking for magic rings or tracking Gollum in the woods. I learned that Tolkien had written more, but this was before Amazon, so finding books was a chore. When I was ten, I found *The Silmarillion* in a library, read it, and lost it while we were in one of our periods of semi-homelessness. The librarian kindly told me to go ahead and keep the book if it turned up, since no one took it out anyway. Eventually I found it, and still have it, but my first copies of the trilogy are long read to tatters.

By the time I was a teenager, Tolkien's universe felt as familiar as, and often preferable to, my own. Trying to adjust to social expectations as a homeschooler in thrift-store clothes who lived in a haunted-looking house with no television or running water was difficult. Often, I was lonely. Sometimes I was bullied. On a few occasions I physically fought the bullies. Between this, and being blond, and riding horses, and pining for unattainable men, I identified with Eowyn, all the way.

But I didn't analyze *The Lord of the Rings*. I just tried to live in it. Middle-earth, to me, wasn't a made-up place, but an alternate reality. I even resisted learning about Tolkien, feeling he got in the way of his work. When I finally read Peter S. Beagle's introduction to the Ballantine edition, I found words for what I'd been feeling:

> For in the end it is Middle-earth and its dwellers that we love, not Tolkien's considerable gifts in showing it to us. I said once that the world he charts was there long before him, and I still believe it. He is a great enough magician to tap our most common nightmares, daydreams and twilight fancies, but he never invented them either: he found them a place to live, a green alternative to each day's madness here in a poisoned world. We are raised to honor all the wrong explorers and discoverers—thieves planting flags, murderers carrying crosses. Let us at last praise the colonizers of dreams.[1]

Even having learned about Tolkien's life and scholarship, even knowing that he identified with the hobbits himself, I still pretend he was a wizard who had figured out the secret of traveling through worlds, and had brought us dispatches from one of them.

---

[1] J. R. R. Tolkien, *The Lord of the Rings,* intro. Peter S. Beagle (Boston: Houghton Mifflin Co., 2004), 935.

JOHN RONALD REUEL TOLKIEN was born in 1892 in South Africa, where his father, Arthur Reuel Tolkien, managed a bank. When he was three, his father died, and his mother, Mabel (née Suffield), moved her family back to England, settling in Worcestershire, which would later lend some of its attributes to the Shire. Shortly after their move, Mabel converted to Catholicism, against the wishes of her family. When she died of diabetes in 1904, she left Tolkien and his younger brother in the guardianship of a close friend and Catholic priest, Francis Xavier Morgan.

While in his teens, Tolkien became interested in languages. He also met and fell in love with Edith Bratt, of whom his guardian disapproved, as she was three years his senior, and a Protestant. But in 1913, while studying English language and literature at Oxford, the two became engaged. The following year, when England entered World War II, Tolkien joined an infantry regiment and while still in training, in 1916, married Bratt.

A few months later, he was sent to France to fight in the Somme Offensive, one of the deadliest battles in history. Shortly after he was invalided home with trench fever, nearly everyone in his battalion was killed. Though Tolkien rarely spoke of his time in the Great War, it influenced his writing. His grandson, Simon Tolkien, in an article for BBC, writes that "evil in Middle Earth is above all industrialised. Sauron's orcs are brutalised workers; Saruman has 'a mind of metal and wheels'; and the desolate moonscapes of Mordor and Isengard are eerily reminiscent of the no man's land of 1916."[2] The aftermath of the war also shaped Tolkien's perspective. His grandson writes: "There is a sense too that the world has been fundamentally changed by Sauron even though he has been defeated." Frodo, like a combat veteran, emerges scarred and traumatized, unable to be at peace, even in his beloved Shire.

During his convalescence, Tolkien began writing his first stories, which were eventually published as *The Book of Lost Tales*. In 1920, he took a post teaching English at the University of Leeds, but after five years he returned to Oxford, where he taught until his retirement in 1959. During his time there he wrote *The Hobbit* and the first two books of *The Lord of the Rings*. As well as creating the lore of Middle-earth, Tolkien was a philologist and translator. His translations of *Beowulf* and *Sir Gawain and the Green Knight* are highly regarded, and he was popular as a lecturer. A man of scholarly but playful temperament, devoted to his wife and children, Tolkien found it odd, in the final years of his life, to be a popular icon, and on one occasion referred to his hippie fans as his "deplorable cultus." He died of a chest infection at age eighty-one, in September 1973, and before he could see a different set of deplorables come along and claim him.

---

[2] Simon Tolkien, "Tolkien's Grandson on How WW1 Inspired *The Lord of the Rings*," BBC website, January 3, 2017.

Who owns Middle-earth?

I can't talk about revisiting Tolkien in the way I revisited Chesterton, because I never really left him. Over the years I have ducked back into his world from time to time, finding new perspectives on the stories, though I never studied Tolkien in a class, or taught him. In my undergraduate years, conservative academics refused to take Tolkien seriously because they couldn't accept fantasy as real literature. But at some point this changed. Conservative Christians stopped looking askance at Tolkien and began to accept him, then celebrate him. And, despite Tolkien's notorious detestation of allegory, began identifying Christ figures and Christian symbols.

One of the biggest issues with interpreting Tolkien is that his work has ballooned into such a vast cultural phenomenon, between the movies and fan theories and popular disputes and scholarly interpretations, it can be a challenge to brush it all aside and get back to the texts themselves. Tolkien scholar Verlyn Flieger writes about discovering *The Lord of the Rings* back in 1956 ("those were the days"), noting that it is different now. "The growing body of writing both by and about Tolkien ensures that not only can we no longer read the unknown book I discovered in 1956, we can't even all read the same book in 2019," she writes. "We have too many opinions based on too much information from too many sources to come to a consensus."[3] Whether the concept of canon is

---

[3] Verlyn Flieger, "The Arch and the Keystone," in *Mythlore: A Journal of J. R. R. Tolkien, C. S. Lewis, Charles Williams, and Mythopoeic Literature* 38, no. 1, art. 3 (October 2019).

helpful for elucidating Tolkien's work is debatable. The website Tolkien Gateway has a nuanced policy on this, noting that "canon is a concept which cannot be uniformly applied to J. R. R. Tolkien's legendarium." Scholar Corey Olsen of the Mythgard Institute, responding to controversy over *The Rings of Power*, takes it further, claiming that there's no such thing as canon in Tolkien's work at all, since the author was constantly playing around with his creations, and sometimes creating conflicting storylines. I like this idea for two reasons. One, it feels like we're talking about a real universe, so maybe I will find my way to Middle-earth someday. Two, it means Tolkien can never be reduced to a conservative culture-war icon.

But the far-right obsession with Tolkien remains. And it's not a new thing, either. Tolkien's first superfans in the United States may have been the hippies, but in Italy in the 1970s they were folk-fascists associated with the New Right. This group opposed progressive values but distanced themselves from Mussolini's futuristic fascism. And they were obsessed with Tolkien. They organized outdoor festivals involving music and teach-ins called Camp Hobbit where people could get back to the land, learn about Middle-earth, and be indoctrinated into white supremacy. Giorgia Meloni, a neo-fascist with anti-immigrant and antisemitic views who became prime minister in 2022, was introduced to Tolkien at these events and has been obsessed with him ever since. More recently, in 2017, far-right leaders in Italy organized Camp Hobbit 40, to celebrate the fortieth anniversary of the original festival.

I'd like to say that the far right completely misreads Tolkien, but there are aspects of the stories that fit a little too neatly into their ideologies: the obsession with the local, the predominantly patriarchal social structures, the almost entirely male cast of characters. The association of North and West with good, South and East with bad. The racially coded character descriptions. The romanticization of kingship and a hierarchical social structure.

Tolkien's fondness for the local may seem appealing, but localism by itself is a faulty framework. When not balanced with a sense of global connectivity and responsibility, it can morph into xenophobia and nationalism, even fascism. An extreme instance of this is eco-fascism, a far-right version of environmentalism that seeks to preserve natural resources for the "superior" race.

ANOTHER FORM IS THE natural-living trend in conservative Christian subcultures. Here, otherwise wholesome practices around local sourcing get entangled with a fixation on purity that manifests itself in traditional gender roles, anti-science conspiracy theories, and a demonization of sexual minorities and ethnic outsiders. We see this in the trad-wife movement and in anti-vaxx signaling. I observed this trajectory among my "crunchy con" acquaintances and some of my fellow farmers' market vendors and wrote about it for *The Christian Century* in 2021. Kathleen Belew discussed a similar phenomenon in a 2022 essay for *The Atlantic*, "The-Crunchy-to-Alt-Right Pipeline."

A Tolkien-inspired aesthetic permeates the domestic side of this trad-wife, anti-vaxx subculture, where images of adorable kitchens and children wearing natural fibers are curated for social media to evoke a hobbit-hole quaintness. Yet the xenophobic politics of the traditionalist movement undercut the seeming wholesomeness of the aesthetic, as far right localists weaponize Tolkien to argue against immigration. In 2019, the ultra-conservative Catholic magazine *Crisis* published a piece stoking fear about Muslims in Britain titled "Sauron Comes to Middle England." In a 2024 article for *Gilbert: The Magazine of the Society of G. K. Chesterton,* Joe Grabowski argued that "the Shire, really had been what the Hobbits were fighting for all along."[4] The pro-nature aspect of traditionalist movements is also undermined by the voting habits of this demographic. Making sourdough and composting while voting to remove environmental protections and drill on public lands is like professing to admire Sam Gamgee while cheering on Saruman—as long as he stays out of our backyard.

On one hand, I think Tolkien would hate this reduction of his vision. His localism, fervent though it was, was not insular. In his stories, love of home is balanced with longing to explore the wide world and see its wonders. Bilbo wants his comfortable hobbit hole but also wants to see mountains again. Plus, in Tolkien's stories, survival often depends on the ability to make allegiances outside one's kind. Unexpected

---

[4] Joe Grabowski, "A Lesson in Localism," *Gilbert: The Magazine of the Society of G. K. Chesterton* 27, no. 6 (July/August 2024).

friendships arise, such as between Bilbo and Balin, or Legolas and Gimli. Whoever you are, hobbit, elf, or ent, you can't hope to protect your beloved home without working for the safety of the homes of others. Localism must be tempered with care about the wider world. Otherwise, Frodo could just toss the Ring into the Brandywine River and spend the rest of his days peacefully in Bag End.

Yet I have to face the reality that Tolkien's writings lend themselves to these xenophobic uses. There's Tolkien's clear preference for cultures that mimic Western Europe, his representation of Southern and Eastern ethnicities as dangerous and foreign. There's the passage early in *The Fellowship of the Ring* where a sinister traveler at The Prancing Pony warns that refugees from the troubles in the South will soon be arriving in Bree: "If room isn't found for them, they'll find it for themselves," he says.[5] The traveler is described as "squint-eyed," and the concept of "outsiders" is framed as threatening.

Tolkien and supremacy narratives

Tolkien's descriptions are frequently racially coded in this way. He describes the orcs as "slant eyed, "dark," and "swart." The saga of Middle-earth is also heavily race based, with conversations about race and blood running through the whole of *The Lord of the Rings*. The "pure" Numenorean blood has

---

[5] Tolkien, *The Lord of the Rings*, 172.

been diluted, which means they lack the longevity of their ancestors. As Faramir explains to Frodo and Sam, in *The Two Towers*: "For so we reckon Men in our lore, calling them the High, or Men of the West, which were Númenoreans; and the Middle Peoples, Men of the Twilight, such as are the Rohirrim and their kin that dwell still far in the North; and the Wild, the Men of Darkness."[6] Racial coding comes up again here, since the men of Harad and other Southern and Eastern ethnic groups, who ally with Sauron, have "dark faces" and "black eyes," and rise against the noble Northern groups that are either explicitly white (the Rohirrim) or generally taken to be white (the people of Gondor).

Going back to Flieger's point that Middle-earth belongs to no one and everyone, we can argue the right of any reader to imagine hobbits, elves, and the rest with whatever racial coding they prefer. And yes, there are gray areas allowing for racially diverse depictions. We can point to the description of hobbits as having brownish skin and eyes, and curly hair, or the thesis that Tolkien was partially inspired by Jewish culture in his envisioning of Numenor. And why not depict elves as ethnically diverse? Their only consistent physical traits are that they are taller and better-looking than the average human. This work to untether Tolkien from white supremacy is being done. Search Google for "racially diverse Tolkien art" and you'll find Black Aragorn, Native American Celebrimbor, and multiple beautiful non-white elves. Amazon's *The*

---

[6] Tolkien, 704.

Rings of Power series also broke past the white coding with its racially diverse cast—and received intense backlash from angry Tolkien fans.

Or we can point out, against the white-supremacist readings, that in Tolkien's universe, the Numenoreans' obsession over their "superior" lineage is presented as a weakness that brought about their doom. We can remind the xenophobes that, in the trilogy, the hope of beating Sauron depends on different peoples managing to unite and leave their divisions behind. Or that Tolkien's ultimate heroes are not the ones with the impressive pedigrees, but people like Frodo and Sam. Greatness is not about ethnicity or lineage, but about moral choices.

Tolkien's defenders often point out that he opposed the apartheid regime in South Africa and loathed Hitler's regime. When the Nazis wanted to translate *The Hobbit* into German, and asked him to prove his "Aryan blood," Tolkien said he would rather not have the translation done on those terms. "I have many Jewish friends," he wrote to his publisher, "and should regret giving any colour to the notion that I subscribed to the wholly pernicious and unscientific race-doctrine." To the Nazis he wrote: "If I am to understand that you are enquiring whether I am of Jewish origin, I can only reply that I regret that I appear to have no ancestors of that gifted people."[7]

This is commendable but doesn't erase the racialized depictions in his stories. Readers who are not white, reading

---

[7] J. R. R. Tolkien, *The Letters of J. R. R. Tolkien*, ed. Humphrey Carpenter (Boston: Mariner Books, 2000).

certain passages, get the message that these stories are not for them. Which is, of course, precisely the way far-right fans want them to feel. So even though there are pathways out of white-supremacist readings of Tolkien, those who take them have work to do, not just because of the pushback from right-wing Tolkien fans, but because the problematic racial coding is real.

Tolkien's depiction of the orcs as an inherently evil and inferior species is also frequently brought up as evidence of his racism. It could be argued that the orcs are not technically a race, but a genetically altered species, since Sauron created them by torturing and warping elves. Race or not, depicting an entire humanoid people as morally irredeemable is dangerous, since such ideas have been used to justify various forms of oppression, even genocide. Tolkien scholar Tom Shippey has suggested that the orcs were created as an enemy that can be killed without compunction—a horrifying implication—something that likely came from Tolkien's nightmarish experience of war and the uneasy celebration of the glory of a war between humans. The scene in *The Two Towers* when Sam sees the face of the dead Southern warrior offers that sense of post-wartime internal conflict Tolkien may have carried:

> It was Sam's first view of a battle of Men against Men, and he did not like it much. He was glad that he could not see the dead face. He wondered

what the man's name was and where he came from; and if he was really evil of heart, or what lies and threats had led him on the long march from home; and if he would not really rather stayed there in peace.[8]

The Rings of Power series raised questions about this idea that orcs are really beyond redemption (another idea that got extreme pushback from fans), reminding viewers that these beings, unlovely though they are, are also victims: created to be slaves, now perpetual exiles, unable to live in the sun, only seeking a home of their own. Tolkien himself is very clear that in his view the creator made all things good. No one was ever evil from the start, and evil itself can only deform, never create.

Knights, patriarchs, and kings

In *The Lord of the Rings*, kingship has a mystical significance, so Aragorn is not just a political hero; as king he wields a sacramental power, like that of the rings themselves. He can take possession of the palantir, command the dead, and heal the wounded. On his own, Aragorn is a splendid argument for kingship. But Aragorn is make-believe. And even in Middle-earth, the history of Numenor stands as a warning to any who would claim the crown. Aragorn has to rise above the errors

---

[8]Tolkien, *The Lord of the Rings*, 687.

of his ancestors, not just in resisting the temptation of the ring, but also in refraining from pride, arrogance, and lording it over his subjects. Aragorn's ruling style, which makes sense given his broad and diverse kingdom, is pretty hands off. He's definitely not forcing everyone to conform to the same culture or religion. Tolkien once said that his own political views tended toward either anarchy or unconstitutional monarchy, and maybe Aragorn's kingship is how Tolkien envisioned his idiosyncratic political ideal.

Then there's the patriarchy issue. Very few female characters appear in Tolkien's stories. There are no women at all in *The Hobbit,* and only a few in *The Lord of the Rings.* The three who are most significant are Arwen, Galadriel, and Eowyn, and of these only Eowyn seems like a real person, with conflicts and a character arc. Galadriel, though a powerful queen who has done mighty deeds, remains enclosed within Lothlorien, the traditional lady in her chaste garden. Arwen, too, remains enclosed, a prize to be won by the hero once he's fulfilled his quest. Both even do traditional "women's work" of weaving. Critic Melissa McCrory Hatcher notes: "Hobbit women are mentioned, but only as housewives or shrews, like Rosie Cotton or Lobelia Sackville-Baggins. Tom Bombadil's wife Goldberry is a mystical washer-woman. Dwarf women are androgynous, while the Ents have lost their wives."[9]

Tolkien, like other male writers, could create heroic and powerful women, be a kind husband, but still be sexist. When

---

[9] Melissa McCrory Hatcher, "Finding Woman's Role in *The Lord of the Rings.*" *Mythlore* 25, no. 3 (2007).

Tolkien describes his mother's suffering in the last years of her life he calls her a "martyr" who "killed herself with labour and trouble to ensure us keeping the faith." This tribute, though born out of love and gratitude, is disturbing. Why is he so ready to accept this appeal to martyrdom and excuse women's suffering related to a "righteous" end? Tolkien doesn't stray far from the church where mothers' lives are valued lightly, even while they are honored for their sacrifices.

Tolkien was a far better husband and father than Waugh or Greene, and he and Edith were generally happy together—at home. However, she was not a part of his academic or literary worlds, and resented this exclusion. Maybe Edith inspired Eowyn's complaint to Aragorn: "All your words are but to say: you are a woman, and your part is in the house. But when the men have died in battle and honour you have leave to be burned in the house, for the men will need it no more." Later, when Eowyn's brother Eomer expresses his perplexity at her malady following her injury in battle, Gandalf says:

> My friend, you had horses, and deed of arms, and the free fields; but she, being born in the body of a maid, had a spirit and courage at least the match of yours. Yet she was doomed to wait upon an old man, whom she loved as a father, and watch him falling into a mean dishonoured dotage; and her part seemed to her more ignoble than that of the staff he leaned on.[10]

---

[10] Tolkien, *The Lord of the Rings*, 901.

Strange that Tolkien could write a compelling argument on behalf of women's equality, yet not put it into practice in his own life or even find a way to make that argument with consistency in his writing. "Tolkien probably was the stodgy sexist Oxford professor that feminist scholars paint him out to be," critic Hatcher writes.[11]

Tolkien leaves his women on the margins, with the suggestion that there is more to their stories, but in most cases, those stories are never told. As a Catholic, Tolkien was heir to a tradition that simultaneously reveres women and dehumanizes them. Women can be pure maidens, self-giving mothers, holy saints, but never leaders, never ministers of divine power. And the only perfect woman, Mary of Nazareth, manages to be both virgin and mother—something impossible for ordinary everyday women to imitate. Despite multiple claims that Catholics can't be sexist because they venerate Mary, the church has often weaponized Mary, as well as women saints, against us living, imperfect women with our messy lives. Perhaps the ambiguities in this tradition explain why Tolkien's women are both powerful and marginalized, intriguing yet underdeveloped. Feminist readers can and should claim space in Tolkien's world and do the work to fill in what's neglected in his women characters—we don't have to feel that we are barred from his world just because some angry sexists would like to keep us out. Unfortunately, however, there are reasons why the angry sexists feel uniquely entitled to Middle-earth.

---

[11] Hatcher, "Finding Woman's Role in *The Lord of the Rings*."

"Everyone has their own private Tolkien," Flieger notes.[12] And, I'll add, no one's private Tolkien is the magisterial Tolkien. Because my private Tolkien was a refuge and comfort for me for most of my life, I've sometimes resisted coming to terms with the reality that he wove certain prejudices into his work. One of the biggest challenges of deconstruction can mean admitting that artifacts or traditions we love are flawed and that the benefits we derive from them are not available to others in the same way. Those of us who love and value Tolkien's stories have an obligation both to admit this, and to admit that no matter what work we do to take down those barriers, some may remain. Many readers may prefer to find refuge in stories that don't dehumanize or sideline them.

At the same time, Tolkien's world is also bigger than his prejudices. And we can honor everything that's good in it by continuing to push back against those who try to reduce it to its worst and weakest attributes.

In the story of the rings of power, one of the perils of the One Ring is that it tempts people to overstep their bounds and claim domination. Those who want to make Middle-earth the exclusive domain of white, conservative, heterosexual Christians are falling prey to this temptation. They are trying to plant their flag in Middle-earth, but this is impossible. The moment anyone tries to seize it, it ceases to be Middle-earth. And while all of us can journey there,

---

[12] Flieger, "The Arch and the Keystone."

it's up to us to decide who we'll be in the story. Do we take the Ring and use it to dominate, destroy, and exclude? Or do we accept that one little corner of the Shire is enough to grow our gardens on?

10

Flannery O'Connor

The O'Connor mythos

I almost wish Flannery O'Connor had never become popular among Christians. This is not a comment on the quality of her stories or the value of O'Connor scholarship. But the mythos that the Christian literary subculture has constructed around her sometimes obscures her reality as a person, and as a writer. Conversations about her work easily slide into predictable patterns, so we're talking less about her stories, more about what people have told us to think about her stories.

When I was introduced to O'Connor in my late teens, it was in an academic culture that had already decided what she meant. Before I had a chance to explore her acerbic humor or incisive style, and certainly before I had a chance to ponder her depictions of race, I was handed a set of ready-made interpretations, and dutifully handed back my carefully drafted theses about the sacramental imagination and the violent intrusion of divine grace. Knowing that O'Connor's stories were intended to shock an apathetic culture, it never occurred to me that maybe mine was the culture that needed to be shocked.

It's kind of fun to imagine an alternate timeline, where O'Connor's work remained obscure for decades, where there was no mythos enshrouding her, and we only just discovered her, with no hagiographical trappings. How would we react? Hopefully, we would still recognize her tremendous artistic gift. But her most pious fans might be offended by her depictions of devout Christians, and progressives less than charmed by her depictions of race.

The importance of religion in her work, I don't think anyone could miss. Just as reading *The Odyssey* means understanding how the Homeric era viewed its gods, reading O'Connor well demands engagement with her faith. In this respect, Christian scholars, especially Catholics, have an advantage, being already at home within her imaginative framework. But maybe we also have a disadvantage, since it's so easy for us to linger over religious themes to the neglect of others. It doesn't help that Catholics have anointed O'Connor as our literary patron saint, so we tend to make excuses for her when she writes things that are problematic.

Besides her Catholic faith, her illness and her identity as a Southerner are also essential for talking about her stories. But here, a clarification: O'Connor's Southerness needs to be qualified with the adjectives *white* and *middle class*. Her perspective is only one of many possible Southern ones, and even though she writes about Black and poor white Southerners, she doesn't speak to them. Flannery O'Connor does not tell the Southern story, she tells a white Southern story.

MARY FLANNERY O'CONNOR, THE only child of Edward Francis O'Connor and Regina Cline, was born on March 25, 1925, in Savannah, Georgia. The house they lived in is located in the historic district of the city, close by the Cathedral of St. John the Baptist, and is now a museum, free and open to the public. In 1940, the family moved to Milledgeville, Georgia. A year later, her father died of lupus.

O'Connor studied English literature and sociology at the Georgia College and State University (then called the Georgia State College for Women), where she also worked as a cartoonist for the student newspaper. After graduating from an accelerated program in 1945, she went on to the Iowa Writers' Workshop at the University of Iowa, initially to study journalism. During her time in the program, she had the chance to study with several highly regarded writers, including Robert Penn Warren, John Crowe Ransom, and Andrew Lytle, all Southerners like herself and associated with the Southern Agrarian literary movement.

After earning her MFA from the University of Iowa in 1947, she received a fellowship that enabled her to stay on for one more year. She spent the summer of 1948 at an artists' community in Saratoga Springs, New York, and also spent time with classicist and translator Robert Fitzgerald and his wife, Sally, in Connecticut, before moving back to Georgia. She and her mother relocated to Andalusia, a farm near Milledgeville, in 1951. A year later O'Connor was diagnosed with the same disease that had killed her father. For twelve more years she lived on at Andalusia, writing stories, corresponding with friends, and raising peacocks, as her health continued to deteriorate. She was only thirty-nine when she died.

Disability and the grotesque

O'Connor's experience of her father's illness, and later her own, shaped her perspective on bodies. Even her descriptions of clothing highlight the awkward futility of our choices in physical adornment. In "Everything That Rises Must Converge," an older, racist, white woman justifies her purchase of an overpriced green and purple hat, saying, "At least I won't meet myself coming and going."[1] But on the bus, a Black woman sits down across from her, wearing the same hat—which, by the way, is gaudy and hideous. Physicality itself, in O'Connor's imagination, exists in the realm of the grotesque, and she focuses particularly on bodies that don't conform to standards of typicality: tattooed bodies, disabled bodies, fat bodies, wounded bodies, intersex bodies, self-mutilated bodies.

---

[1] Flannery O'Connor, "Everything That Rises Must Converge," in *Three by Flannery O'Connor: Wise Blood/the Violent Bear It Away/Everything That Rises/Must Converge* (New York: Signet Classic, 1986), 272.

Since her focus is on society's outsiders, readers often refer to her characters as freaks and her stories as a freak show. Lisa Oliverio, in an article on disability in O'Connor's fiction, writes, "The disabled figure presents a mirror for all of humanity's spiritual brokenness in a fallen world."[2] But this is a classic case of the ableism of treating unconventional bodies as symbols of moral or spiritual perversion. Even if O'Connor's "freaks" and outsiders are mediators of grace, this still reduces them to a narrative commodity, as though they have to point to something other than themselves to have value.

O'Connor wrote most of these stories while experiencing hereditary sickness and disability herself, however—a fact that has captured the imagination of the literary community. "It was the illness I think that made her the writer that she is," said author Alice McDermott. I am a bit uneasy with this claim. Yes, sickness offered O'Connor unique perspectives, and her disability is important for understanding her work. The tortured genius trope usually focuses on artists with mental illness, like Vincent van Gogh or Sylvia Plath, but we also have a fascination with terminally ill or physically disabled artists, like John Keats or Frieda Kahlo. But the trope is problematic. Plenty of people experience debilitating pain or trauma without ever translating it into art, and others create excellent art while living relatively pain-free lives. Romanticizing pain can be, frankly, dangerous. When we believe suffering generates beauty, we absolve ourselves of the

---

[2] Lisa Oliverio, "Disability in Flannery O'Connor's Fiction," *Interdisciplinary Journal of the Dedicated Semester* 2 (2011).

obligation to do anything about it. We treat someone's pain as a useful commodity producing beauty for us to enjoy. As Poppy Burton writes in an essay for *Far Out* magazine, most of our favorite "tortured artists" had their careers cut short by their own suffering.[3]

BUT CREATIVE WORK CAN still be especially empowering for those who are limited in other ways, whether through physical confinement, disability, or disenfranchisement. We can resist ableist readings of O'Connor's sickness but still recognize how she drew on her experiences of disability in her work, and how her art became especially important to her, as other options for exploration diminished. When she learned she had lupus she expressed relief, not because she welcomed sickness, but because she'd known something was wrong but wasn't sure what. "I thought I was going crazy," she told her friend Sally Fitzgerald. "And I'd a lot rather be sick than crazy." But she suffered. She lost her hair, her face swelled, she had difficulty moving her limbs and had to use crutches. Yet she continued writing until the very end, determined to finish her final story, "Revelation," before she died. Maggie Levantovskaya, writing from the perspective of someone with lupus herself, notes that "there's a romance to the image of O'Connor as a nerdy, sickly woman who pushed on, writing about violence and death. The contrast is powerful. I knew all of this without

---

[3] Poppy Burton, "Everything Wrong with the 'Tortured Artist' Trope," *Far Out,* July 30, 2023.

having read her work. Her importance as a writer with lupus was hard to ignore."[4]

The racism problem

Levantovskaya sought out O'Connor's work because of their shared illness, and found a stoic, sardonic approach to her chronic condition, a "resilience without delusion." But she found something else, that came between her and O'Connor: racism. "She gave me language I could've used," Levantovskaya writes. "But that language does not exist in a vacuum. It is surrounded by other language—words that were and continue to be used to repress Black freedom for the benefit of white supremacy."

O'Connor's treatment of race has haunted discourse on O'Connor for decades, but few critics have addressed it directly. Angela Alaimo O'Donnell's book *Radical Ambivalence: Race in Flannery O'Connor*[5] brought the topic into the spotlight for all to see. Anyone who, noting certain of O'Connor's word choices (including her liberal use of the "n-word"), wonders how racist she was, can find an answer in this book, especially through details from private correspondences that were conveniently left out of previous publications

[4] Maggie Levantovskaya, "On Flannery O'Connor's Chronic Illness . . . and Chronic Racism," *Literary Hub,* August 6, 2020.
[5] Angela Alaimo O'Donnell, *Radical Ambivalence: Race in Flannery O'Connor* (New York: Fordham University Press, 2020).

of O'Connor's writings. O'Donnell includes them. And they demonstrate that O'Connor was quite racist indeed.

O'Connor opposed segregation only reluctantly, favoring a gradualist approach that wouldn't upset white Southern sensibilities. She wrote that she was an integrationist by principle but a segregationist by taste. "I don't like negroes," she wrote in a letter. "They all give me a pain and the more of them I see, the less and less I like them. Particularly the new kind." Presumably the "old kind" were the ones who kept to the places to which a white supremacist society had assigned them. She seemed to have a particular animus against James Baldwin. "About the Negroes, the kind I don't like is the philosophizing prophesying pontificating kind, the James Baldwin kind," she wrote in a letter to her friend Maryat Lee, another Southern writer, who was a queer woman and a progressive feminist. In another letter to Lee she states that she would be willing to meet with Baldwin in New York, but not in Georgia, since "it would cause the greatest trouble and disturbance and disunion." She also spoke dismissively of Martin Luther King, Jr., and made racist jokes.

Though O'Connor's racism was pretty much on a par with that of other polite white Southerners of her era, O'Donnell argues that she was willing to grapple with this moral failure in herself. "In her stories her better angel often ruled, as she worked hard at representing the relationship between the races justly, trying not to let her personal feelings and antipathies intervene," O'Donnell notes. But she also acknowledges that "her whiteness sometimes prevented her from doing so."[6]

Some white conservative Catholics still refuse to see this, however, and insist that O'Connor was not racist, or that, if she was, it wasn't a big deal. Mark Bosco, SJ, writing for *America* magazine, refers to O'Connor's statement about not liking negroes as "transgressive humor, playing the country bumpkin to Lee's Yankee liberal."[7] There's no evidence that O'Connor's remarks about Black Americans, in her private letters, were intended to be tongue-in-cheek, and if the goal was to be humorous, it falls flat. Transgressive humor is real, but only works when it punches up, at powerful oppressors, not down, at the vulnerable. She was not play-acting as a stereotypical white supremacist in those letters. She was being one.

White discourse

In 2020, after Loyola University Maryland removed O'Connor's name from a dormitory that had been named after her, O'Donnell criticized this choice in an article for *Commonweal*, arguing that O'Connor should not be "canceled," since white readers can learn from her internal

---

[6] Angela Alaimo O'Donnell, "The Moment in Race Relations That Keeps Repeating Itself," *Church Life Journal,* May 12, 2020.

[7] Mark Bosco, SJ, "Flannery O'Connor: A Walking Contradiction on Race," *America,* July 17, 2020.

struggles with her own latent racism. In my own conservative university, no one encouraged us to read O'Connor this way. The issue of race was usually ignored. I recall one teacher presenting O'Connor as a champion of racial justice because of her critiques of bigoted white Southerners. We could have benefited, in our programs, from some teachers willing to be honest about O'Connor's views on race. The last time I taught O'Connor in a college classroom, I tried to take an approach like the one O'Donnell suggests, using these stories as a space within which we white readers could confront our own ingrained prejudices.

For instance, in "Everything That Rises Must Converge" the liberal main character, Julian, purports to be antiracist, mostly to annoy his bigoted mother. White people today who are inclined to center themselves as allies or coopt the language of antiracism to assert moral superiority can learn from seeing themselves in this unpleasant character, who even goes so far as to plot to date a Black woman for the sole purpose of goading his mother. As a white man, Julian feels entitled to use Black women's bodies as props or weapons in his intergenerational dispute.

Yet this pedagogical method is only relevant for white readers encountering O'Connor in predominantly white spaces. Sociologist Tia Noelle Pratt, responding to O'Donnell in an article also in *Commonweal*, helped me appreciate this. Pratt points out that Loyola University renamed the building in question Thea Bowman Hall, honoring the singer, writer, and activist who was the first Black member of the Franciscan

Sisters of Perpetual Adoration, and who is on track to potential sainthood. Pratt writes:

> Even though I am a lifelong Catholic, and O'Connor is a prominent figure in Catholic literature, it was always clear her work wasn't for or about me. Perhaps that is why I wasn't interested in it. Yet, as a Black Catholic woman, I have always been expected to see myself in white spaces because Catholicism in the United States was, and in many ways still is, synonymous with whiteness.[8]

Pratt's perspective is illuminating here. This isn't to say that Black readers can't appreciate O'Connor (both Toni Morrison and Alice Walker admired O'Connor's writing). But most of the conversation around O'Connor and race, in Catholic literary culture, is a very white discussion, among predominantly white people. Black readers are already aware that white liberals tend to sideline or appropriate from nonwhite cultures, so they're clear there is no invitation to Black readers here. Meanwhile, O'Connor does the same thing she lampoons in Julian. The Black characters in "Everything That Rises Must Converge" do not appear as human beings, but as props to make a point. And O'Connor uses racially problematic stereotyping in her description of the Black woman, emphasizing both her largeness and her sullenness, describing

---

[8]Tia Noelle Pratt, "I Bring Myself, My Black Self," *Commonweal*, November 3, 2020.

her as a "giant," and describing the "downward tilt of her large lower lip."[9] The woman speaks only to shout at her child, until the very end, when the white woman offends her by offering the boy a penny, at which point the Black mother hits the white one with her pocketbook. This scene may have been intended to convey divine retribution but looks more like a white supremacist designation of Black people as violent and reactive. The mother has a stroke. Julian learns a lesson. The Black woman was just a vehicle for their moral betterment.

Racial justice? Maybe later

O'Connor's final story, "Revelation," depicts the cosmic, theological jolt to a smug white woman when she realizes the implications of the gospel. Mrs. Turpin spent her entire life thinking well of herself as a good Christian and literally shouts with gratitude that God didn't make her like any of the classes she looks down on. A violent encounter with a mentally disturbed young woman shakes her out of this spiritual complacency. "Go back to hell where you came from, you old wart hog," the girl said to her. And she can't shake these words. The girl's name is Mary Grace, some in-your-face symbolism from O'Connor that connects with Mrs. Turpin's conviction that the insult was a message from God. And she resents it. "If you like trash better, go get yourself some trash, then," she rails at God. At the story's end, Mrs. Turpin is

---

[9] O'Connor, "Everything That Rises Must Converge," 280.

granted a vision: she sees "a vast horde of souls were tumbling toward heaven." At the head of the procession are the people Mrs. Turpin has despised—poor whites, Black people, "battalions of freaks and lunatics shouting and clapping and leaping like frogs." At the end of the procession are the people like herself, "marching behind the others with great dignity, accountable as they had always been for good order and common sense and respectable behavior. They alone were on key. Yet she could see by their shocked and altered faces even their virtues were being burned away."[10]

It's a vivid illustration of "the last will be first," which, to follow O'Donnell, was likely O'Connor attempting to confront her own prejudices in the final days of her life, in the last story she ever wrote. Yet Mrs. Turpin's vision, striking though it is, does not truly image the justice of God's kingdom. For one thing, humanity remains segregated, and designations of "freak" and "lunatic," foisted onto society's outcasts, remain, even in the afterlife. Nor does O'Connor really question the virtues of the polite white Christians; she only imagines them being "burned away."

Profound as the vision in "Revelation" is, it fails to get at the heart of the Beatitudes. The point of this cosmic reversal, where the last become first and the first become last, is not some ineffable mystery whereby God, for reasons we can never fully understand in this life, reverses our expectations. God does not simply upend human designs to remind us to

---

[10] Flannery O'Connor, "Revelation," in *Three by Flannery O'Connor*, 423.

stay humble. The reversal of the Beatitudes is not gnosis. It is justice. The respectable people are sent to the end of the line not simply because God's ways are not our ways but because our ways, which privilege the powerful and give a pass to oppressors, are unjust and immoral. Maybe O'Connor did grasp this, vaguely; if the virtues of the nice respectable white people burn away, perhaps it's because they were fake, cardboard virtues from the start.

But the inadequacy of the vision in "Revelation" helps make sense of the fact that O'Connor, though willing to contemplate a reversal of caste structure in heaven, resisted racial justice movements on earth. If we don't truly believe that white supremacy is evil, an assault not just on the order of heaven but on the order of natural rights, it's easy to sit back and say "Oh, it will all be resolved in the afterlife." O'Connor was willing to assent with her mind to the truth that white supremacy is contrary to God's plan. But she was raised in a deeply racist culture, which saturated her moral consciousness. It seems unlikely that she managed to purge herself of it, even at the end. Maybe she could have, if she'd had the guts to go meet with James Baldwin or take a real stand for the oppressed.

The problem with white Christian literary culture

Pratt's assertion that Catholicism in the United States is still mostly synonymous with whiteness is also true about much of Christian literary culture, which has often excused or even upheld white supremacist assumptions. Rereading O'Connor now, I notice things I did not notice twenty or even ten years ago. And the reason I did not notice them is that I was educated in a culture of white supremacy. I could call it "polite" white supremacy, or "nonviolent" white supremacy, but the work of white supremacy is neither polite nor nonviolent.

Reading in a white supremacist culture didn't rule out including the occasional Black writer on our reading lists, or listening to famous Black writers talk about their craft. We did those things. We were also willing to speak disparagingly of enslavers and the kind of overt, "impolite" white supremacy depicted in some fiction. But much of this was done with an air of patting ourselves on the back, as though, having added Toni Morrison to a reading list, or attended a talk by Derek Walcott, we'd done enough.

The Catholic university where I did my doctoral work treated O'Connor and her literary mentors—the Southern Agrarians and the Fugitives—as icons. Much of the literature we read was by Southern writers, most of them white, who used stories to reevaluate their culture's dominant narratives. We deconstructed the "Lost Cause" propaganda that tried to reinvent the defeated Southern enslavers as noble, downtrodden heroes who had just made a little mistake. We contrasted Faulkner's gritty depictions of the South with the "moonlight and magnolias" version in *Gone with the Wind*. But for the most part we skirted around the full evil of the Confederacy, keeping our focus less on the stories of the enslaved African

Americans of the South, and more on the guilt of the white
Southerners and their failed war. Southern culture, in those
conversations, always meant white Southern culture. And
when we talked about the evil of slavery, we referenced the
South's "tragic flaw," as though it were a magnificent, noble,
lofty civilization that just happened to make that unfortunate
little error of trafficking, enslaving, abusing, raping, and torturing millions of Black Africans. So Black Southern writers,
though we took them seriously as artists, remained marginal
to the central drama of educated white Southerners torment-
ing themselves over their "flaw."

This was my personal experience, but it wasn't just mine.
The program I was in has produced many Christian scholars,
and some of them, today, are associated with far-right or white
supremacist ideologies. And while white Christian literary
culture has progressed, we haven't sufficiently addressed our
failures to reckon with our own legacy, or to do atonement for
the structural sins that we carry. It's more pleasant to pretend
we were brave and antiracist all along. But we weren't.

And how brave was O'Connor? Her fans talk about her
as though she was a solitary but heroic prophet, forcing an
indifferent world to witness the truth about good and evil.
Veronica A. Arntz, writing for *Faith and Culture: The Journal
of the Augustine Institute,* asserts that "to our softened, modern
sensibilities, the stories of Flannery O'Connor are shocking."[11]

---

[11] Veronica Arntz, "Grace and the Grotesque: Redemption in the
Southern Literature of Flannery O'Connor," *Faith and Culture: The Journal
of the Augustine Institute* (June 28, 2018).

Perhaps they are shocking to more sheltered readers, but the literary world today has seen it all. And in an era where the headlines tell of brutal violence and climate catastrophe, are we shocked by a story about a family murdered on a road trip, or a woman gored by a bull? Or consider the era O'Connor lived and wrote in. A decade earlier, World War II claimed the lives of some forty million people, the Germans murdered six million Jewish people, and the United States used nuclear weapons to kill tens of thousands of Japanese civilians. In the "Christ haunted" American South, white vigilantes brutalized and murdered Black people. In 1955, the same year O'Connor published her short story collection *A Good Man Is Hard to Find*, three adult white males in Mississippi abducted, tortured, and murdered fourteen-year-old Emmett Till, because a white woman claimed he had whistled at her.

Yet polite white society turned away from all this, just as polite white society today refuses to address hate speech, even from our political leaders. So, yes, something needs to shock us. But O'Connor might not be the writer to do this, since she skirts some of the issues that most directly need to be addressed. Many of her fans seem similarly reluctant to name the evils to which they think we need to remain alert. On Bishop Robert Barron's *Word on Fire* website, Lauren Myers, writing about the story "Parker's Back," lists the ideologies that apparently plague modern culture: gender ideology, gnosticism, hedonism, and iconoclasm. Myers names none of the concrete evils that were rampant in O'Connor's culture, or our own. Nothing about abuse, rape, war, genocide, gun violence, deportation, or poverty. Nor does she name the evil ways of thinking that generate these assaults on human dignity: white supremacy, antisemitism, xenophobia, the worship of wealth and power, the technocratic paradigm.

O'Connor similarly avoids directly naming and confronting the evils of her time, and it's difficult for me to envision any reason for this other than that she didn't want to. We know she was capable of being brave, because she faced her lupus bravely. We know she was capable of being direct, because she wrote directly. But, writing at a time when Black writers and activists, along with white allies, were putting their lives on the line, she could not raise her voice to support them. On the matter of racial justice, she was a coward.

O'Connor's stories remain brilliant in many ways. And, as O'Donnell argues, reading them closely and asking the right questions can indeed help white readers interrogate their prejudices. But that doesn't make O'Connor racially non-problematic, let alone a hero of antiracism. She did know something we seem to have forgotten, however: the people who most need to be shocked are often the people who are most comfortable, the ones who occupy power, the ones who have never before had their cheery self-assessments challenged, the Mrs. Turpins of our society, churches, and literary circles.

Is Christian literary culture prepared to take a stand against the evils that afflict our society and harm the most vulnerable among us? I hope so. But in this, O'Connor can only serve as a guide up to a point. If we are going to be real about challenging the evils of our time, white Christian readers, writers, and scholars in general need to be more intentional about learning from both the criticisms of non-white readers and the stories of non-white writers. And we need to be willing to answer a gospel call that Flannery O'Connor, for all her brilliance, refused to hear.

11

Walker Percy

Drunk white male privilege

Suppose I wrote a novel about a middle-aged woman, successful in her career but a disaster in her personal life. Though raised Catholic, she is no longer a church-goer and spends her time drinking heavily and having flings with attractive men half her age. Convinced it is her destiny to prevent an imminent global catastrophe only she can see coming, she stockpiles guns, food, and whiskey in an abandoned motel and holes up there with three young men, two of them her lovers. Despite being drunk much of the time, she manages to stave off disaster, and settles down, in the end, with one of the handsome young men. And maybe she doesn't live happily ever after, but she does okay.

Would the Catholic literary world celebrate this book? Would they adore my messed-up heroine? Likely not. Most

Catholic readers expect a different type of woman protagonist. If she's going to be sympathetic, she should be at least a little like the Virgin Mary, or any of our traditional women saints or heroes. Judith cut off a general's head, but did so while beautiful, sober, virtuous, and devout. Mary of Egypt might have been a prostitute, but she did a lot of penance afterward. In the Catholic imagination, we women are expected to stay on our pedestals, and if we slip off, we should do so in our younger years, so we can fall prettily. But afterward, we must make atonement. Perhaps we could dramatically renounce all hope of happiness in love, like Julia in *Brideshead Revisited*. Or make a penitential pilgrimage and die of the plague, like Kristin Lavransdatter, in Sigrid Undset's novel of that name. If we can't be pretty, we need to justify our existence by being wise, motherly, patient, and dutiful. A drunk, out-of-shape, philandering, middle-aged woman would have to pay for her misdeeds to earn the approval of Christian readers.

Flip the gender script, however, and you have the plot of Walker Percy's 1971 speculative satire *Love in the Ruins: The Adventures of a Bad Catholic at a Time Near the End of the World*. When I read it in my early twenties, I found it profound and hilarious; now, I find it mostly self-indulgent.

THE PROTAGONIST OF *LOVE in the Ruins*, like most of Percy's protagonists, is a white male of respected family and relative access to wealth, who is having an existential crisis. Dr. Tom More, a remote descendent of St. Thomas More, is a psychiatrist living in a country club community in Louisiana, in a near-future as imagined by the author in the 1960s. Civilization is falling apart. Things break and are not repaired. Vines grow on everything. Political and racial polarization have become extreme, and young people are dropping out of society, smoking weed, and practicing free love. Christian militia-like groups band together. Black Power–type groups gather in the swamplands. Liberals suffer from anxiety and impotence, while conservatives suffer from rage and constipation.

As a vision of society on the brink of collapse it's pretty mild, but it's a fascinating look at some of the fears of the well-off white Catholic male in the contemporary United States. The cars will not start! The center will not hold! All this polarization! Plus, people keep hooking up and having meaningless, depraved sex. It's all so empty and hedonistic at the same time, it makes Dr. More sad, and the only solace for his sadness is to fornicate himself, though when he does, it isn't depraved; it is poetic and meaningful. Today, over fifty years later, well-off white Christians plagued by similar worries inevitably point to Percy's novel as prescient.

And in some respects, it is. For instance, in Percy's future dystopia, the "American Catholic Church" has split from Rome and dedicated itself to property rights, patriotism, and racism. And even if the raging conservative and anxious liberal are caricatures, they are rooted in a familiar reality. I have met the anxious educated liberals and apoplectic golfing conservatives and even the men who frown at sexual shenanigans while seeking them out on the sly.

The luxury of an existential crisis

Early in the novel, Dr. More ponders the specter of societal collapse, and muses over what's behind it. He sincerely believes that the United States was ordained by God to save the world, and he has been elected to save the United States. His vision of history is essentially Manifest Destiny: God chose the "lordly Westerners," granting them "Israel and Greece and science and art and the lordship of the earth."[1] But then, More imagines, God tested the nation. The test? "Here's a helpless man in Africa, all you have to do is not violate him." Obviously, the nation failed the test.

But More isn't satisfied with the idea that white supremacy is our real original sin. His search for the spiritual ailment behind this moral failure yields the conclusion that the real problem is Cartesian dualism: the separation of the physical from the spiritual, human alienation. It's a familiar complaint conservative academics make, talking about poor Descartes as though he had literally separated mind from body. So, is More theorizing that white people enslaved and oppressed Black people because Descartes posited a radical separation of mind from body? It sounds ludicrous, but there's something to it. A society that believes the body doesn't matter will happily commit any number of atrocities, sometimes even in the name of spiritual betterment. Even today some Christians defend chattel slavery and colonization with the

---

[1] Walker Percy, *Love in the Ruins* (New York: Farrar, Straus and Giroux, 1971), 57.

argument that it "brought Jesus to the heathens." But putting the blame on Descartes is unfair. People were denying the importance of the body and brutalizing one another long before modernity came along.

In the story, Dr. More has invented, almost by accident, a device called an Ontological Lapsometer, which can diagnose and treat this spiritual ailment of mind/body separation. Unfortunately, his device has fallen into the hands of a strange, unsettling character, Art Immelmann, who has the vibe of a seedy traveling salesman but is actually the devil. Is he there to tempt Dr. More to succumb to pride and pleasure? Or is his goal to accelerate catastrophe? Maybe both. Many ribald and violent events unfold, and at the last minute, More realizes what is happening and calls upon St. Thomas More to assist him. Immelmann disappears in a puff of smoke and the crisis is averted.

If More were a woman, he'd be expected to repent and atone after this, deny himself like Julia, die of pneumonia like Sarah Miles—but he is a man, so all he has to do is be a little humbler, accept that it is not his destiny to save the world, give up on trying to fix humanity with his lapsometer, and learn to muddle along even while feeling anxious and alienated. His punishment is that he must accept the human condition.

Love in the Ruins is the most action packed of Percy's plots, the most like a popular novel. But its thematic concern, the crisis of human alienation, is the primary focus of all Percy's writing. His philosophical questions are similar to those of the European existentialists, but with a Catholic angle and a Southern twist. And it works. I, at any rate, accept that the rational response to finding yourself on the grounds of a golf course at a racist country club in the American South is to sink into Sartrean nausea or Kierkegaardian despair. Percy really is good at highlighting the pitiful absurdity of our little quests to fill the void within, whether with golf tournaments or white-lady faux spirituality.

At the same time, More's despair in the face of golf courses and spiritualism is self-indulgent. The world of letters is saturated with meditations on the emptiness of a life spent in pursuit of enjoyment. Middle-aged professors feel angst and embark on affairs with students. David Foster Wallace writes about the miseries of a pleasure cruise in "A Supposedly Fun Thing I'll Never Do Again." The overarching message is that we become restless when we are too comfortable, unhappy when disconnected from nature. Or maybe it's the conscience pricking us because we are fiddling while people starve, and cities burn. It's an existential crisis reserved for the privileged.

One cure for the crisis is to have that comfort stripped away. To be forced back into the struggle to survive. Percy is aware of this, and so is Dr. More. When a patient suffering from impotence consults him, More advises him to walk the six miles home through dangerous swampland instead of taking the carpool. After slogging through muck, being chased by alligators, and sniped at by guerrillas, the patient stumbles home and makes "lusty love" to his wife. Making lusty love is a big deal for Percy. It's how the abstracted, tormented male can regain contact with reality. Women are merely the conduits for existential reentry.

Despite the limitations of his perspective, Percy's depictions of existential unmooring are frequently believable. And given his own personal experiences of pain and loss, he's not just skimming the surface of human emotions.

The doctor in search of a cure

Walker Percy was born on May 28, 1916, in Birmingham, Alabama, into an old Southern family whose forebears included LeRoy Pope Walker, the first secretary of war for the Confederacy. The Percy family line was marked by depression, trauma, and multiple suicides. In 1917, Percy's grandfather shot himself in the head. Twelve years later, when Percy was thirteen, his father did the same. And two years after that, his mother drove her car off a bridge and died. Though this was not ruled an act of suicide, Percy suspected she intended to take her own life.

Percy and his two younger brothers were taken in by his father's cousin, William Alexander Percy, who was a lawyer, a scholar, and a Catholic. Thanks in part to the influence of "Uncle Will," Percy developed an interest in books and ideas. As a teenager he became friends with Shelby Foote, who would later be celebrated as an amateur historian of the South.

He and Foote both attended the University of North Carolina at Chapel Hill, where Percy majored in chemistry and wrote for the university's literary magazine. In 1937, he graduated and went on to study medicine at Columbia University.

Shortly after starting an internship at Bellevue Hospital, Percy contracted tuberculosis while performing an autopsy and had to quit. During the next few years, while his brothers fought in the Second World War, Percy recuperated, reading extensively, especially in the European existentialist tradition. His views on science, religion, and human life began to shift, so that while he continued to take science seriously, he no longer viewed it as the answer to life's pressing dilemmas. Believing something more spiritual was needed, to address the problem of fundamental alienation, Percy began to think more seriously about religion in general, and to be drawn to Catholicism in particular. It was during this time that he began attending mass.

In 1946, Percy married Mary Bernice Townsend, a medical technician, and soon afterward, along with Townsend, entered the Catholic Church. They had two daughters, the first of whom was adopted. The Percy family settled in Covington, Louisiana, near New Orleans. Percy never went back to practicing medicine but had an active career as a writer, teacher, and literary mentor, prior to his death from prostate cancer in May 1990.

Percy launched his career as a Catholic writer with an essay in *Commonweal* about Southern stoicism, Christianity, and racism. In 1961, he made his novelistic debut with *The*

Moviegoer. In 1966, he published *The Last Gentleman,* and introduced the character of Will Barrett, who would later appear in his 1980 novel *The Second Coming,* which also details the existential crisis of a middle-aged white professional male who finds himself through a sexual relationship with a much younger woman.

In *The Second Coming,* Will is afflicted by the onslaught of memory and convinced that life has no meaning. So, he decides to put God to the test by deliberately getting lost in a cave. If God exists, he reasons, God will save him. He ends up falling out of the cave into the secret shelter of a young woman who has escaped from a mental institution and, thanks to shock therapy, has no memory of the past. What happens next will surprise no one.

In 1977, Percy published his bleakest novel, *Lancelot,* which takes the reader into the head of a morose lawyer, Lancelot Lamar, who is obsessed with the idea of sexual innocence and is institutionalized after killing his daughter, his wife, and their lovers in a mass-murder event. This is another novel that invites the reader into the mind of a disturbed individual.

What's even more unnerving about *Lancelot* is that Percy seems to assume that the reader will agree with his demented protagonist's assumptions about the world, women, and sexuality. In his other novels Percy seems to write partially to convince himself. In *Love in the Ruins,* he's reminding himself to settle down and stop having a God complex. And his audience of well-off white men probably needs the same reminder. So even while eye-rolling at some of Dr. More's observations, I can still see where he's coming from. I too have despaired on a golf course. I too have tried to test God.

But what's the point of *Lancelot*? Once I would have argued that he's just doing the same thing Nabokov did in *Lolita,* inviting us to enter the psyche of a disturbed person in order to reckon with the human capacity for vileness. Now, I am not so sure. I have to wonder whether Percy sympathized with Lancelot Lamar and expected his Christian readers to sympathize as well. Because I've seen too many of my fellow Christians embrace ideologies of hatred unnervingly adjacent to Lancelot Lamar's obsessions. Percy almost seems to be trying to convince himself, through the character of the common-sensical priest Percival, that radical terrorism is not the solution. So much energy is poured into depicting the hate, so little into offering a cure.

Percy's final novel, *The Thanatos Syndrome*, published in 1987, brings back Dr. Tom More, on a mission to save the world again, this time from a conspiracy of scientists who are dispensing with the elderly via euthanasia, while sexually abusing children. On one hand, *The Thanatos Syndrome* could be viewed as just a prelude to twenty-first century conservative conspiracy theories like Pizzagate or QAnon, or mass hysteria about cabals of sinister scientists putting microchips in vaccines. On the other hand, the dystopian future Percy depicts in this novel isn't wholly the stuff of paranoia, given our culture's indifference to the sick and vulnerable, and the very real epidemics of human trafficking and sex abuse.

False narratives

Unlike O'Connor, Percy is explicit in his discussion of the moral quandaries of the modern world. Also unlike her, he eventually realized that gradualism was not the way to end segregation. He spoke openly about it, to the point that he was targeted by the Ku Klux Klan. His willingness to change his mind and take a stand is admirable. Yet his approach to racial justice remains rooted in white supremacy: Western culture is superior. White Western Man (and he does mean Man, in the gendered way) hubristically mucked everything up, and now must sweep in and be the savior. Like Atticus Finch from *To Kill a Mockingbird,* Percy opposes an unjust system that does violence to Black people. Like Atticus, he is willing to take a stand. But also, like Atticus, Percy holds onto white supremacist notions.

In *Love in the Ruins,* Percy persists in depicting the struggle for racial justice as a "both sides" issue: angry white golfers and angry Black guerrillas just need to learn to live peaceably with each other. His view of slavery as a test for white Christians dehumanizes Black people, reducing them to objects in a cosmic moral examination. The lordly white male is the main character. The rest of us are props.

As readers we are encouraged to view More as more enlightened than the other white men in the country-club set. He treats Black patients. He opposes violence against Black people. He also uses racial slurs. Even when articulating his views on the sin of chattel slavery, More does so through racist language, including the "n-word." Yes, this is a white Southern man created in 1971 by another white Southern man. Yes, that's how some people talked and still talk. But More—an educated, sophisticated man (even if grubby from trysting in motels and crawling in ditches)—ought to know better. Later, we find him telling the leader of the Black guerrillas, patronizingly, that he won't succeed in achieving peace and brotherhood until he's gotten to where the white people are. "And I'm not even sure you can do that," he adds.[2] More adorns his American exceptionalism with blatant anti-Asian racism, too: "As bad as we were, there was no one else, and everyone knew it, even our enemies, and that is why they curse us. Who curses the Chinese? Who ever imagined the Chinese were blessed by God and asked to save the world? Who ever expected anything else from them than what they did? What a laugh."[3]

You could argue that Percy writes More this way because More is a weak character and we're supposed to roll our eyes at him. But there's no evidence that More is supposed to repent of his nationalistic or racial hubris, even after he's been humbled. And why would there be? Both Percy and More refer to the Christian tradition as the arbiter of their moral sense. This tradition, for centuries, had severe words for sexual sinners while remaining silent or complicit in matters of racism, white supremacy, and chattel slavery. And the white

---

[2] Percy, 373.
[3] Percy, 57–58.

Christian literary world inherited that complicity and created a canon around it.

Percy's *Commonweal* essay, "Stoicism in the South," is an excellent example of how a fractured ethic leads to a false narrative. The essay paints a picture of the American South similar to that propounded by the Southern academics I studied with years ago; that is, the slaveholding South was a great, but tragically flawed culture, ruled by a noble upper class committed to the classical virtues, especially the ideals of the Stoics. "The greatness of the South, like the greatness of the English squirearchy, had always a stronger Greek flavor than it ever had a Christian," Percy writes.[4] And herein, he believes, lies the problem. Stoicism alone, Percy argues, is not a strong enough elixir to motivate the aristocratic Southerners to work for justice.

Percy's diagnosis once again is flawed. Yes, the white ruling class of the American South failed catastrophically to live out even the most basic Christian precepts. And certainly, some erudite Southerners were enamored of the Classics, Percy's "Uncle Will," included. But the idea that Southern plantation owners failed to be Christian because they were too dedicated to a classical, Stoic value system is incredibly off base. Chattel slavery was not built on Stoicism. Nor were the articles of secession. And while slavery was deeply embedded in the culture of the ancient Greeks and Romans, white Christians in the Americas managed to make the practice

---

[4] Walker Percy, "Stoicism in the South," *Commonweal*, July 6, 1956.

even more brutal and dehumanizing. "They were just too Stoic to help it" is a ridiculous claim.

In both his *Commonweal* piece of 1956 and his novel of fifteen years later, Percy perpetuates a useful fantasy that can help educated white Southerners feel better about their history. When writing about the supposed *noblesse oblige* of white landowning Southerners, Percy refers, not to historical documents, but to characters from Faulkner's novels, made-up people bursting with sensitivity and fine feelings. He claims that "until a few years ago the champion of Negro rights in the South, and of fairmindedness and toleration in general, was the upper-class white Southerner"[5]—an assertion that is simply false. Not only is it unsupported by historical evidence; it's in direct contradiction of it. But this idea, that the aristocratic white Southerners were the finest allies of Black Southerners, is one of many post-slavery myths in the intricate edifice of "Lost Cause" propaganda.

As Caroline E. Janney points out in *Remembering the Civil War: Reunion and the Limits of Reconciliation,* white Southerners, after the war, told a variety of inaccurate and often conflicting stories in order to exonerate themselves. One of these was the myth of the happy, faithful slave, loyal to the white enslaver. Another was the romanticized image of the South as a peaceful agrarian society.[6]

---

[5] Percy, "Stoicism in the South."

[6] Caroline E. Janney, *Remembering the Civil War: Reunion and the Limits of Reconciliation* (Chapel Hill: The University of North Carolina Press, 2013), 211.

Here's the true story: In many areas of the South, it was the poor white sharecroppers who allied with Black people to work for expanded civil and property rights. In North Carolina, between 1894 and 1900, the movement of Fusion Politics arose when poor farmers organized across racial lines to free themselves from debt and servitude to wealthy merchants and larger landowners. In West Virginia coal country, in 1921, when the United Mine Workers of America organized the Miners March that led to the Battle of Blair Mountain, both Black and white laborers joined forces against company officers and police. The battle, which lasted from August 25 to September 2, remains the largest armed encounter to take place on US soil since the Civil War. And in Tyronza, Arkansas, in 1934, Black and white tenant farmers allied against the landowners and formed the Southern Tenant Farmers Union. The laboring classes, not the ruling classes, were more likely to promote Black liberation.

Percy also buys into the myth that Reconstruction was oppressive to white Southerners, and refers to it, in his *Commonweal* essay, as "one of the most shameful occupations in history."[7] This melodramatic piece of Lost Cause propaganda was debunked as early as 1935, by W. E. B. DuBois in *Black Reconstruction in America: An Essay Toward a History of the Part Which Black Folk Played in the Attempt to Reconstruct Democracy in America, 1860–1880.* Today, historians of the Civil War side with DuBois. The story of Reconstruction as a terrible op-

---

[7] Percy, "Stoicism in the South."

pression of white Southerners is not a reputable thesis. It was an invention of the Dunning School (named for Columbia University professor William Archibald Dunning), which supported conservative ideologies and opposed civil rights.

Reconstruction failed not because it was too aggressive, but because it was too soft. Heather Cox Richardson argues in *How the South Won the Civil War* that the oligarchic, conservative, and hierarchical South triumphed in ideology, even if it lost the war. So here we have the intellectual and moderate Walker Percy ignoring historical facts but repeating Lost Cause propaganda in the pages of liberal *Commonweal* in the 1950s. Years later I heard the same propaganda in the lecture halls of a Catholic university.

Too few readers or critics seem inclined to challenge these myths. Yes, we've come a long way. Yes, progressive Christian literary culture is now committed to including diverse voices and perspectives. But I'm not sure we can create a truly equitable literary or academic culture without reckoning more seriously with the falsehoods and moral wrongs woven into our literary legacy. We can't just pretend that white supremacy wasn't happening in the pages of our most beloved books. We can't pretend some of our own mentors didn't abet it.

The lordly male

In the case of Percy, as with others in the Christian literary canon, we need to reckon with his sexism also. Throughout his novels, Percy reduces women to objects. In *Love in the Ruins,* Dr. More's overweening ambitions are presented sympathetically. But when one of his love interests talks about entering music competitions or taking her horse to shows, More gets impatient. Ambitions are for men. Women are meant, not to strive, but to support the strivers. The woman More finally marries is fiercely loyal to him, but trash-talks the other two women refuging in the motel, judging them for their promiscuity, while refusing to judge More for his. She, of course, has "saved herself for marriage." She's not like other girls.

Rereading *Love in the Ruins*, while I found myself mostly rolling my eyes, occasionally I nodded along. Percy really is brilliant when it comes to capturing the absurdity of life in modern America. He's better at observation than diagnosis. One of his best books is his nonfiction work *Lost in the Cosmos,* a parody of the self-help genre that brilliantly and hilariously captures the ironies of the anxieties and despairs of the hyper-aware. You can read it, ask the questions, then work out the problems yourself. Percy's diagnoses of the ailments of America may be wrong, but I think he does look at the evil of chattel slavery and ask why. And I agree with him that the Christian doctrine of original sin offers a framework. It is a thesis that remains general and allegorical, and it emerges from a creation myth that puts the blame on the woman, but it's still a useful starting point for telling the story of human history.

From the perspective of a writer, trying to figure out where and how to start a story is always a challenge. We go back to a character's childhood, looking for a trigger or a memory. But we could go back forever, following the chain of human trauma and endurance, so the storyteller has to choose a moment. Percy chooses to start his novel with Dr. Tom More breaking out in hives in a grove of pines near the interstate, but knows the story begins earlier, in a remote past beyond our reach. All good novelists know part of the task of telling the story is the task of asking, What led to this? And what comes later? I don't agree with Percy's answers, but appreciate that he asks the questions. They're the same ones I keep asking: How did we go so wrong?

Part Three

Tactics for Reading

12

How We Read Matters

Virtuous readers?

As a teenager, I liked to quote Oscar Wilde: "There is no such thing as a moral or an immoral book. Books are well written, or badly written. That is all." I don't think I believed that completely (Wilde probably didn't, either); it was my response to conservatives who policed my reading based on subject matter. I still agree with Wilde that ethical principles aren't the only ones that matter when we assess literature. Aesthetics also matter, and not just as ornamentation. Craft, structure, rhetoric, and style matter. And the purpose of reading is much bigger than simply the development of virtue.

At the same time, ethical values are important. Christian literary culture tends to stress this, arguing for a robust literary education as valuable for the formation of virtue. This is the premise behind books like Jessica Hooten Wilson's *The*

Scandal of Holiness: Renewing Your Imagination in the Company of Literary Saints, and Karen Swallow Prior's *On Reading Well: Finding the Good Life through Great Books*. And I think they have a point. The literature we consume does shape our understanding of ourselves, our relationships, and our place in history. The literature a culture elevates shapes the culture. So even if Wilde is right that art itself is never moral or immoral, this doesn't mean our choices in reading are morally irrelevant. One reason why the books we celebrated in our traditionalist reading cultures failed to make us the good people we were supposed to be is that we read books that advanced false, harmful ideas.

The other reason was that we read them in a culture that wasn't about to encourage us to critique those ideas. I would have had very different experiences of Chesterton, Eliot, Waugh, and the rest had I read them in classes and with teachers who encouraged me to critique their presuppositions about human nature. Once I moved on to a university that identified as conservative but with a classically liberal component, there was more room for asking the kinds of questions I needed to ask—questions about the ethical parameters around relationships, when violence is or isn't legitimate, how different cultures should interact with one another, how to balance faith practice with religious tolerance, and what it means to be a truly just society.

Conservative academic culture has become even more extreme, less willing to engage in dialogue, more hostile to any scholarship that doesn't confirm its preexisting beliefs.

Certain Catholic universities have become the intellectual branch of burgeoning fascism. Some of the institutions that promoted a classical liberal approach to the humanities twenty years ago now openly promote a far-right message. At the time of my writing this, the reactionary fringe has become so mainstream that it's influencing national and global policy. So it is all the more crucial to think seriously about the literary education of white Western Christians. What are we reading, and how are we reading it? And how should those of us in the Christian literary world respond to the challenges of this time?

Many thought leaders in the Christian literary world are strong proponents of social and racial justice, leading important conversations about how to deal with things like antisemitism in Chesterton or racism in Flannery O'Connor. We're seeing more diversity in our lineups of Christian writers and scholars. That's great, but we still have a long way to go.

A toxic culture

One problem is that Christian literary culture persists in thinking of itself as a bastion of virtue in the face of evil secularism, talking about our artistic offerings as though we are uniquely positioned to evangelize the culture and bring truth to a benighted world. It's a nice idea, but it simply isn't true. Given white Christianity's complicity in evil movements past and present, we should be a lot more humble about our influence on the world. We should be taking a stance, not of triumphalism, but of penitence.

Additionally, we've let our lopsided Christian ethos shape our sense of what a Christian imagination even is. In my own Catholic literary culture, there's a lot of talk about such theological themes as hope, redemption, sacramentality, and grace, and much less concern about liberation, justice, the preferential option for the poor, and communal sin—the values that threaten empires. And our books reflect this. But this doesn't make them bad books. It's just that our relationship with these books has become unhealthy, insufficiently critical, prone to hero worship.

Our tendency toward culture-war cliquishness is also a problem. We're too willing to give a pass to those who can check the "Christian writer" box, regardless of any bad behavior they may have engaged in, or bad ideas they might promote. When I look at a list of speakers at any Christian literary event, I am curious about two things. How hard have they worked to bring in writers from different backgrounds, ethnicities, and experiences? But also, have they platformed the kind of people who, simply by being present, make that space less safe for those minority writers? Have they brought in speakers with a history of abusive behavior, who have affiliated with problematic groups, who have spread hate about marginalized populations? It's essential that we be mature enough to sustain diverse viewpoints, but there's a limit to this. Predatory behavior or bigoted speech are not in the same category as, say, a disagreement over whether Waugh's

Catholicism was sincere, or how to interpret disability in O'Connor. Including marginalized writers is necessary, but the effort is self-defeating if they're included alongside those who denigrate them.

Kaya Oakes, in her 2024 book *Not So Sorry: Abusers, False Apologies, and the Limits of Forgiveness,* writes about how Christians tend to privilege powerful abusers, and demand forgiveness from their victims. When powerful persons, especially straight white men, are caught doing something bad, usually all that's expected of them are a few displays of tearful regret, and everyone rushes to rehabilitate them. This happens in literary establishments as well; people find excuses for problematic figures, not just the ones who are long dead, but people who wield power at universities and in publishing. Several prestigious poetry journals (*Rattle, Tupelo Quarterly*) are presently helmed by men who, though credibly accused of abusive, sexist, or racist behavior, continue to enjoy prestige in their field. So Christian literary establishments are doubly prone to forgiving abusers, silencing survivors, and rehabilitating problematic characters. If a writer has a history of inappropriate behavior toward women, there's nothing noble about looking past this and inviting that person to a conference. If others associate with racist organizations, or write homophobic content, including them alongside Black and queer speakers isn't diversity. It's toxicity.

A truly equitable culture that reflects gospel values requires we be less eager to hand out cheap forgiveness, and less reverential about our problematic favorites. It's not a cancellation to put these writers under a microscope instead of on a pedestal. It's a necessity, if we want to read problematic literature for the sake of the value these works still have.

So it's not just what we read that's important, it's how we read. We should be competent to identify rhetorical techniques and understand how they affect us, to identify when good ideas are tangled up with bad ones, to differentiate between personal taste and artistic value. And we need the self-possession not to be swayed by writers' views just because we love their work, or because they fit our previous conceptions.

A critical toolkit

In the world of publishing, writers are encouraged to seek out sensitivity or authenticity readers, if they plan on writing about subjects that fall outside their range of experience, especially if marginalized identities are involved. Some writers resent this as a form of censorship, or complain that, if it's fiction, why should they worry about having to be accurate? Resistance to sensitivity readers may be more common among conservative-leaning writers, but the idea that good artists need to consult no one but their personal muse is not just a right-wing thing; it's typical of modern Western civilization in general—myself included.

Admitting that we benefit from an expert perspective other than our own requires humility. This can be a challenge for writers, especially, since this is such a private, solitary art form. But realistically, no one creates art in a vacuum. Even the most introverted, misanthropic writer is still a part of a community, creating art that will be experienced in a community. Consulting a sensitivity reader can be a practice of humility that allows us to grow as a writers, shifting our thinking from a monolithic approach toward a more polyphonic, intertextual one. Readers, especially those in privileged demographics, can benefit from the tactics of sensitivity readers as well.

Drawing on some of these tactics and reflecting on things I wish I'd been aware of as an early reader, I've tried to develop specific habits for reading more ethically, and more intelligently.

1. Consider your relationship with privilege.

Consider the status of your own demographic, in your culture. This requires honesty—not calling yourself oppressed just because someone criticized you once. It also means thinking intersectionally, paying attention to multiple experiences or identity markers, and how they influence one another. You might have fewer resources due to geography or finances but still have relative privilege based on race, ability, or appearance. Why is this important for reading? You should know whether your culture is likely to privilege characters like yourself, or whether you're the target audience. A story you enjoy might be less pleasant, or even genuinely painful, for other readers. I expect the men who chide feminists for having no sense of humor, since we aren't delighted by sexist commentary from male writers, wouldn't enjoy reading a book in which all the main characters are women, the men show up only as eye candy, and the narrator regularly makes derogatory comments about them.

2. Be aware of your preexisting sympathies.

Being honest about your own advantages and sympathies can help you be more objective when you read for character. Are you more inclined to side with characters like yourself? Do you have prejudices or sympathies that influence your reading? Do you unconsciously prefer characters who are more conventionally physically attractive, or judge characters by their body size or type? Do you automatically assume that people of your own ethnicity, social class, or religious background are the good guys? Note how you respond when people like yourself are depicted unfavorably. Maybe your annoyance is justified. Maybe your own demographic is being dehumanized. But if you occupy a position of privilege, maybe you're annoyed because you're not used to being criticized.

3. Look to the margins.

I would have experienced these books differently if I had read them in a subculture that wasn't already predominantly white, patriarchal, and homophobic. The people who were being demeaned in the books we read were not always there to defend themselves. My own experience of feeling I couldn't complain about misogyny or antisemitism is revealing; people in minority demographics won't always speak up when they know they're going to encounter hostility. So it's helpful to ask: Who's missing from the story? How would this story or poem sound to them?

4. Punch up, not down.

Christianity, as conservatives like to remind us, is not about being nice. There is a place for severity and judgment in both Hebrew and Christian scripture. But the judgment is always against the privileged who oppress the marginalized. Does our literature reflect this? If you aren't in the demographics being demonized, you might not notice when something presented to you as funny might actually be toxic. "A bruised reed he will not break, and a smoldering wick he will not snuff out," says the Gospel of Matthew. Good Christian literature should challenge powerful oppressors and lift up those who are cast down.

5. Beware of "single stories."

In her 2009 TED Talk, Nigerian writer Chimamanda Ngozi Adichie talked about the danger of having a single story about people, places, or things. She describes going to university in the United States, and having her roommate make certain assumptions about her: that she listened to "tribal music" or didn't know how to use a stove. "My roommate had a single story of Africa: a single story of catastrophe," Adichie explains. "In this single story, there was no possibility of

Africans being similar to her in any way, no possibility of feelings more complex than pity, no possibility of a connection as human equals."[1] Consider, when reading, whether the author has embraced a "single story" about gender identity, poverty, Blackness, disability. The story the author is telling may not be false or demeaning, but it still might not be the only, the best, or the truest story—or the story people would choose to tell about themselves.

6. Pay attention to language.

Hopefully you'll notice if an author uses an obvious slur, as Chesterton does sometimes. It might be presented, as in O'Connor, as regional accuracy, but even then, it's important to ask, What's the effect on a marginalized reader when a writer feels entitled to use those words? Slurs can also be more subtle. Note whether the writer draws on caricature to talk about minority demographics. It's fine for a Jewish character to have a big nose or a Black character to have full lips, but when a writer focuses only on those traits, and uses stereotypical language to describe them (hook-nosed or thick-lipped), this is reductionist and racist. Look at clothing and speech patterns. Does the author go out of the way to make a lower-class character speak in comic dialect? Or describe the clothing of Asian people as "exotic"? Note patterns in adjective use: Are minority characters repeatedly presented

---

[1] Chimamanda Ngozi Adichie, "The Danger of a Single Story," TED Talks, 2009.

through adjectives that inspire revulsion, ridicule, or fear? And look at figures of speech: Does a writer repeatedly use food metaphors to describe the appearance of non-white women? This can indicate a reductionist, dehumanizing, or fetishizing perspective. Does a writer use metaphors for wild beasts to talk about people from less developed cultures? Or treat disability as a symbol for sin.

7. *Question your personal authorities.*

Often, when we claim to question authority, this only refers to the authorities we don't respect anyway. If you're agnostic, of course you question the pope. If you're a traditionalist, of course you question scientific innovations. By the time I'd been radicalized to ultra-conservatism, "question authority" referred to people or institutions my subculture regarded as suspect: The government. Scientists. Sociologists. But it didn't mean questioning the magisterium of the Catholic Church, or celebrity priests, or revered professors. Who are your authorities? Do you feel you can question them? Do you automatically give more weight to an argument that came from someone you look up to? Is peer pressure a factor? Do you feel you have to revere some writers if you want to be accepted in your community or advance in your career?

8. *Fact check*

Suspension of disbelief has a dangerous side; that is, once a literary work has enchanted you into accepting it on its own terms, you might let your guard down and accept false claims just because they sound compelling, or because a revered figure made them. Before believing something just because your favorite writer said it, check to see if it's true. This will help prevent the spread of misinformation or prejudice that might be latent in a work because of the writer's preconceptions. Yes, fiction writers write fiction, but it's based on the real world, so make sure they're not giving an inaccurate representation of the real world. If they tell you a certain number of people died in a war, verify. If they tell you more women than men suffer depression, look for data. Get used to not believing things just because you read them in a book, even a good book. This isn't an attack on the writer. Nor is it incompatible with a poetic suspension of disbelief. It's a matter of using your mind responsibly.

9. Be wary of generalizations.

In *That Hideous Strength*, Ransom, among other magisterial pronouncements, asserts that female obedience is an erotic necessity—in other words, that women have to submit to men if they want to be sexually satisfied. This claim has no basis and discloses nothing true about the nature of men and women or sexuality in general. Maybe Lewis is talking out of his usual pre–Joy Davidman sexism, and means "obedience" in a general sense, but there are other clues in the story that suggest that he found domination erotic. In the context of communication and consent, there's nothing inherently wrong with this. Making it a universal mandate, however, is a moral disaster—a blueprint for coercion, abuse, and assault. But a young impressionable reader, who has been told that Lewis is an important Christian thinker, might read those passages and accept Lewis's general claim. Women might be manipulated into thinking they have to accept coercion from men. And men may take from this that they have a right to coerce women. If you're reading along and the author puts a sweeping, general claim about life into the mouth of a narrator or a protagonist, stop and ask whether the universalism of it is justified.

10. Check your emotions.

Plato's critiques of art and poetry, most famously in *The Republic*, rest heavily on his observation that they "water the springs of desire"; art elicits emotions. Sometimes these emotions disclose morally relevant truths, as when a story highlights the reality of injustice. But, as anyone knows who has ever been moved irrationally to tears by a commercial, feelings can be manipulated. So when you find yourself feeling pity, anger, or longing because of something you read, ask yourself whether your response is in proportion to reality, or whether you are being emotionally coerced into loving something you should not love, or hating something you should not hate. That's how *Gone with the Wind* spread Lost Cause propaganda: by conjuring sympathy for the Confederates. Feelings have value, and are essential to our humanity, but people who benefit from social privilege need to check the inclination to treat their own feelings as normative. Feeling grossed out by something doesn't make it morally wrong. Feeling elevated by something doesn't make it morally worthy. Wanting something doesn't mean being entitled to have it.

13

So Why Read These Books?

Breaking up and moving on

Maybe you're expecting me to follow up with an argument that we still need to admire and enjoy every classic work of literature—even those that have been a vehicle for damaging ideas. Well, sorry. It's okay not to love them. It's even okay not to read them.

In her 2024 book *Queering Contemplation* spiritual writer Cassidy Hall describes how, after years of studying the work of Thomas Merton, she discovered some of his homophobic comments. As a queer writer who had long looked to Merton as a spiritual guide, Hall found his remarks painful, but then realized that Merton, for all his wisdom, was clueless about LGBTQ issues. "He hasn't had my experiences, so why should I yield to his wisdom?" Hall asked in an interview with *US Catholic* magazine. "What's so wrong with letting him go? What's so wrong about letting new wisdom rise up?" Merton, she says, would probably want people to move on, instead of treating him like the only contemplative writer of the twentieth century.[1]

Hall's approach to Merton can be a guide for how to deal with other writers who have spun ideologies out of privilege and ignorance. Since the Christian literary tradition already includes many fine writers who offer more diverse viewpoints, profound ethics, and a view to justice, why not shift our focus and center them? The canon is always expanding, and some parts of Christian literary culture are being intentional about this. We can be part of that movement for justice, diversity, and social ethics derived from scripture, while acknowledging that the writers discussed in the previous chapters are good, even great.

In the Gospels, Jesus tells his followers to shake the dust from their sandals in places where they are not welcome. He says they may need to cut ties with their families in order to follow him. He even says he comes to bring, not peace, but a sword. These passages are uncomfortable for those at ease in their current situations, but for those in toxic relationships, Jesus saying to "go ahead, cut ties" might be what they need to hear. And if we can cut ties with living family and friends who have harmed us, we can definitely cut ties with books that harm us, and others, too.

---

[1] Cassidy Hall, *Queering Contemplation* (Minneapolis: Broadleaf Books, 2019); Hall, "A Sideways Glance," *US Catholic* 89, no. 10.

The myth of cancel culture

The Christian classics of the twentieth century tend to focus on the opposite: holding onto things of the past, collecting the fragments of a broken civilization, remaining true to tradition. In terms of historical context, it makes sense that Chesterton and Eliot would turn to tradition as a source of continuity, that Lewis would be suspicious of progress and development, that Sayers would overemphasize class consciousness, that Waugh would let nostalgia fuel an entire novel. These writers lived in times of radical change and upheaval and were steeped in Western Christendom's insistence on tradition, obedience, and loyalty.

It's easy to reframe a stubborn fear of letting go as a kind of fortitude. But letting things go can be healthy and natural. And it's not some terrible affront simply to move on. Most of the time, what we deplore as "cancellation" is a bubble of online outrage that bursts and goes nowhere. People just go back to what they were doing before, including the abusers, who go back to abusing.

Kaya Oakes opens her book *Not So Sorry* with a vignette depicting a woman sifting through books, recognizing the name of an abusive man, comparing notes with another literary friend, and realizing that they'd had similar experiences with the same man—a man who was quickly "rehabilitated" and "forgiven."[2] In a 2019 article for *Time*, Sarah Hagi notes

---

[2] Kaya Oakes, *Not So Sorry: Abusers, False Apologies, and the Limits of Forgiveness* (Minneapolis: Broadleaf Books, 2024).

that after #MeToo, men began to fret that even talking to women could get them canceled. "Only that's not what's happening," she writes. "While some powerful men may not have the status they once did, they have hardly been canceled."[3]

You can see Hagi's point played out across culture. Most of the people who were supposedly canceled are still around and doing fine. J. K. Rowling is likely the most canceled writer alive, but she remains wealthy and influential. Abusive pastors move from one church to the next. Predatory priests go into comfortable retirement. Oakes's vignette immediately resonated for me, because I have been that woman, had those conversations, and at this moment can think of several men in Catholic academia or publishing who lost their jobs due to inappropriate behavior—then popped up somewhere else, all wrongdoing "forgotten," everyone eager to give them a second chance. And I can think of women who risked their reputations to speak out about abusers in literary or religious spaces—and were punished for it. And are still being punished for it. Including by supposed progressives.

When I lost my teaching job in 2017, I received an outpouring of support from close friends and online acquaintances, but many people I'd thought well of remained silent. A few months later, when Minnesota Public Radio cut ties with popular radio personality Garrison Keillor due to multiple allegations of inappropriate sexual conduct, a friend and fellow Catholic sent a personal message of support to Keillor.

[3] Sarah Hagi, "Cancel Culture Is Not Real—At Least Not in the Way People Think," *Time*, November 21, 2019.

My initial emotion, when I heard about this, was perturbation. Had we learned nothing from our church's abuse crisis? From #MeToo? Only later did it hit me: When I was fired, she said nothing in my defense. But she'd gone out of her way to support a powerful man accused of misconduct.

Our world is generally eager to find mercy for the powerful. As Oakes writes in *Not So Sorry:* "In America, forgiveness is closely tied up with power. Culturally powerful people demonize and refuse to forgive the culturally weak, all the while demanding that the weak forgive the powerful without preconditions."[4] When cancellation happens, it usually happens to the less powerful—often to those who raised the alarm about abuse in the first place. Police whistleblowers are often punished, fired, even jailed. People who report unethical behavior at work are often harassed and fired. And we know how it goes for women who speak out about a sexual predator. If there is a problem with cancel culture, maybe the problem is that it doesn't really work. "Rather than panicking that someone might be asked to take a seat," Hagi writes, "we would all do well to consider the people who are actually sidelined: those who lose professional opportunities because of toxic workplaces, who spend years dealing with trauma caused by others' actions, who are made to feel unsafe."[5]

So, no, I don't think we need to worry about our most revered writers suddenly vanishing because we decided to be

---

[4] Oakes, *Not So Sorry,* 20.
[5] Hagi, "Cancel Culture Is Not Real—At Least Not in the Way People Think."

honest about the flaws in their works. As aforementioned, Flannery O'Connor is not going away, and I'm not saying she should. But to echo Cassidy Hall, what's so wrong with letting new writers rise up? Why not let new voices enrich our literary culture?

AT THE SAME TIME, there are plenty of good reasons to read these works. The most basic being because we enjoy them. Maybe not all of them, or all of them in the same way. But just as we don't have to love them, neither do we have to hate them.

The idea that we need to reject all literature that contains anything ethically questionable is simplistic. There is no hard line between problematic and unproblematic literature; it's more like a gradation. Sometimes when I'm reading contemporary literature, I notice little whiffs of racism or ableism. And it's not just a white-guy problem. Celebrated women and minority writers have sometimes turned out to be problematic in a variety of ways. Gabriel Garcia Marquez's novels romanticize rape and sexual abuse of minors. Indigenous writer Sherman Alexie and Saint Lucian poet Derek Walcott both were credibly accused of sexual harassment. Alice Munroe ignored her husband's sexual abuse of her daughter. And Marion Zimmer Bradley molested her own daughter.

The conversation about how to deal with problematic writers is ongoing, but three principles I try to keep in mind are as follows: (1) Ignoring bad stuff is never a viable option. (2) Some readers have serious and legitimate reasons for avoiding certain types of content, and we should respect this. (3) It's still okay to read and enjoy books that contain questionable ideas, as long as you keep the first two principles in mind.

I still enjoy some of Chesterton's work, but with a new wariness. I love Eliot, but prefer him in his depressed, agnostic state. Sayers, I respect greatly, but I don't love Lord Peter as I once did. He's kind of entitled and irritating. Waugh was a terrible person but he's also a brilliant writer, and I would probably have wanted to hang out with him. I admire Greene more now than I did as a conservative. I can't understand how I enjoyed him at all as a conservative. I have learned to love some aspects of Lewis's writing much more fervently than I used to, while finding other aspects facile or ridiculous. Tolkien, I love as much as I ever did, and I seek to read him without minimizing elements of racism and sexism in his work, or denying that his tendency toward localism has become the fuel for conservatives embracing fascist ideology. I find O'Connor brilliant still but am less charmed by her than I once was. Percy, I occasionally have difficulty taking seriously. Maybe some of this has to do with personal taste, but it might also relate to the extent to which the writers in question are problematic.

Even if you don't like any of these writers, you might still need to read them for the purpose of literary education, if that's an area of expertise you are pursuing. If you want to be a scholar of modern Western poetry, you need to read T. S. Eliot. If you want to be an expert on fantasy literature, you need to be familiar with Tolkien. You don't have to love them, but you should still study them. The caveat here is that you should be sure to study them in the context of a broader ethics and justice-based approach to literature.

Christianity without Christ

For deconstructing Christians, rereading formative works can be a practice in self-understanding. How did I manage to be a fanatically devout Catholic while rejecting just about every gospel value? By embracing a form of Christianity that had traveled far from its origins in the teachings of Christ.

In Flannery O'Connor's novel *Wise Blood,* the protagonist Hazel Motes invents his own religion, the "Church of Christ without Christ." In preaching a gospel of self-salvation, Motes is attempting to reclaim a sense of agency after his upbringing with his spiritually abusive fundamentalist grandfather.[6] The Church of Christ without Christ echoes Nietzsche's famous passage in *Die fröhliche Wissenschaft* where he talks about seeing the churches as tombs of a dead God. And Jesus himself warned about a church without Christ:

> "You that are accursed, depart from me into the
> eternal fire prepared for the devil and his angels;

---

[6] Flannery O'Connor, *Wise Blood,* in *Three by Flannery O'Connor: Wise Blood / The Violent Bear it Away / Everything That Rises Must Converge* (New York: Signet Classics, 1982).

for I was hungry and you gave me no food, I was thirsty and you gave me nothing to drink, I was a stranger and you did not welcome me, naked and you did not give me clothing, sick and in prison and you did not visit me." Then they also will answer, "Lord, when was it that we saw you hungry or thirsty or a stranger or naked or sick or in prison, and did not take care of you?" Then he will answer them, "Truly I tell you, just as you did not do it to one of the least of these, you did not do it to me." (Mt 25:41b-45)

What did Christianity mean for these and other white Western Christians? What was it that they felt so compelled to defend against secularism and modernity? At a time of cultural disintegration, Christianity provided structure and identity. And the Christian ethos was exciting, heroic, intellectually demanding, an epic adventure. In her essay collection *The Whimsical Christian,* Sayers writes:

It is the dogma that is the drama—not beautiful phrases, nor comforting sentiments, nor vague aspirations to lovingkindness and uplift, nor the promise of something nice after death—but the terrifying assertion that the same God who made the world, lived in the world and passed through the grave and gate of death. Show that to the heathen, and they may not believe it; but at least they may realize that here is something that a man might be glad to believe.[7]

Sayers's frustration with popular piety was due to her objection to Christianity being made feeble and milquetoast. But what does this version of Christianity have to do with the concrete teachings of the historical Jesus, versus the dogmatic version of Jesus who was developed over several centuries of the early church? I'm not going to go so far as to say that white Western Christianity is a church without Christ. But amid all the talk about sacramentality and adventure and heroism and grace, something crucial is missing, and that something is the heart of the gospel: what we do to the least of these, we do to Jesus. A widely known quotation attributed to a sermon of St. John Chrysostom reminds us: "If you cannot find Christ in the beggar at the church door, you will not find Him in the chalice."

WHERE IS THIS IMAGE of Jesus in the much-vaunted Christian imagination? I've spent months looking at different things people have written about the Christian imagination, or the Catholic imagination. Dana Gioia, in his essay "The Catholic Writer Today," identifies certain qualities that characterize Catholic writers:

> Catholic writers tend to see humanity struggling
> in a fallen world. They combine a longing for

[7] Dorothy L. Sayers, *The Whimsical Christian: Eighteen Essays* (New York: Collier Books, 1978), 27–28.

grace and redemption with a deep sense of human imperfection and sin. Evil exists, but the physical world is not evil. Nature is sacramental, shimmering with signs of sacred things. Indeed, all reality is mysteriously charged with the invisible presence of God. Catholics perceive suffering as redemptive, at least when borne in emulation of Christ's passion and death. Catholics also generally take the long view of things.... Catholicism is also intrinsically communal, a notion that goes far beyond sitting at Mass with the local congregation, extending to a mystical sense of continuity between the living and the dead. Finally, there is a habit of spiritual self-scrutiny and moral examination of conscience— one source of soi-disant Catholic guilt.[8]

I like this account, but more as a description of what makes for good literature than of what makes for Catholic, or Christian literature. Because almost none of these attributes are unique to Catholicism or Christianity. A longing for redemption is also present in Greek and Roman tragedy. So is a sense that evil is real, and that nature is charged with the sacred. Many cultures have viewed suffering as redemptive, which is why some traditionally practiced ritual ordeals. Taking the long view of things is not unique to Christians; Jews did it first. As for the sense of the communal, white

---

[8] Dana Gioia, "The Catholic Writer Today," *First Things*, December 2013.

Western Christians are actually pretty bad at that, compared with various Indigenous cultures. (Though we may be better at angst-ridden self-scrutiny.)

Gioia doesn't fixate on virtue, pointing out that many Catholic writers tend to be the opposite of moralistic. Still, if we look at the virtues our literature is supposed to inculcate, well, many cultures besides Western Christendom have celebrated courage, honor, truthfulness, and temperance. Theologically, even the Christian motif of a dying god is not unique. It's present in Egyptian, Greek, Aztec, and Norse mythologies.

In the white Western church, Christ in the person of the poor and oppressed was pushed to the side. Otherwise, Christians would not have found it so easy to engage in and excuse oppression, colonialism, and enslavement, while amassing wealth and military power. So people who turned to that tradition, while they found a rich wealth of ideas, the "dogma that is the drama," the promise of meaning and redemption, largely missed the crucial values that would have insulated them against the rhetoric of extremism. And we, who looked to them as our guides, missed it too.

Brideshead Revisited would make just as much sense even if Jesus never existed. Chesterton, Eliot, Lewis, and Tolkien, though serious about Jesus and the gospel, have a vision of the world that is intensely hierarchical: kings and queens, masters and servants, codes of conduct, distinctions of gender, social class, race, and nationality. Even in her vision of heaven, O'Connor couldn't bring herself to desegregate society. Greene, though he pushed back against these distinctions, especially in *The Power and the Glory*, is stuck still in a Christian framework that assumes them. The nameless whiskey priest finds he is a better Christian outside the church. What does this say about the church?

Sex-obsessed Christians

One of Christianity's most impressive failures has been its fixation on society's codes of sexual morality, often to the neglect of real sexual ethics, such as "do not rape," and to the neglect of justice issues. White Christians argue that we can't judge people of earlier generations because that would mean holding them to the standards of our time. But one need not be a contemporary feminist to condemn sexual assault. The teachings of Jesus should suffice for that.

Our sexual fixation and moral lopsidedness are reflected in the Christian literary canon. Eliot references scenes of sexual debauchery to depict a society in disarray. The big sins that weigh on Waugh's protagonists all have to do with sex—not with hoarding money, neglecting one's children, or being a social bully. Lewis tries to make society's patriarchal and heteronormative sexual norms into metaphysical verities. Percy frets over sexual libertinism while giving his protagonist permission to be a sexual libertine (for existential reasons).

This fixation on sexual transgressions (including the ones that are merely violations of social norms) works well to distract believers from the evils Jesus warned of.

And the effect of this has not been healthy. Many deconstructing Christians, especially women and LGBTQ+ people, carry trauma from years of sexual shaming. The rhetoric of shame has not been used to hold the powerful accountable. It has been used to make impressionable young people feel guilty for desires, sexual preferences, even for having bodies. When powerful people used their influence to sexually violate the vulnerable, it was often the vulnerable who were blamed. No wonder so many people who are deconstructing, both in the church and outside it, are wary of any talk about guilt or original sin. Yet the rhetoric of shame could have been a powerful force for the good, if it had been used to call abusers and oppressors to repentance.

Readers who were harmed by this lopsided sexual fixation might find it liberating to read some of these books in the Christian literary canon and name the places where they mess up. It helps me to understand my own past mistakes and inaccurate moral assessments when I see Chesterton, Lewis, and Percy pontificate about sex, gender, and relationships. Maybe they were just trying to figure things out themselves, but taking them as sources of wisdom was a recipe for disaster. By doing so I signed onto misogynistic and homophobic ideologies, and stuck with them for so long. Maybe, given that I was taught to regard these men as fonts of wisdom, it was unavoidable that I would have wasted so much moral energy agonizing over things like whether my skirts were long enough, or whether I should go to confession because I laughed at a vulgar joke—instead of holding myself accountable for complicity in real sins against human dignity.

That famous "Catholic guilt" is often about things that are not gravely sinful. I've heard Christian women bemoan their own wickedness because they lost their temper with their husbands. I've even heard Catholics worry that God was punishing them because they dared to space their kids using natural family planning. These are communities in which some healthy guilt over real sins might be beneficial, but the sermons in churches usually direct people to nitpick at the wrong things. Never for covering for abusers in their churches. Never for exploitation of workers. Never for bullying LGBTQ+ youth.

FOR READERS WHO PARTICIPATE in privilege, who are protected by the powers that be, reading the literature of white Western Christianity, with its preferential option for the powerful, can be cause for an examination of conscience. Under the influence of Chesterton, did I participate in racism or antisemitism? Did I see domestic abuse and find convenient ways to ignore it? Under the influence of Waugh, did I put the social codes of the upper classes above any concern for justice? Did I let Tolkien's racial coding validate my racial prejudices? Did O'Connor give me permission to reject racial justice movements, with the excuse that we just need to work on ourselves spiritually, instead of for social change?

Throwing the ring into the fire

I said earlier that maybe we need more narratives about cutting ties and walking away. But we already have them, including in the works of some of these writers.

The idea of renunciation is popular in Christian culture. When we are baptized, we renounce Satan and all his works and pomps and empty promises. People who take religious vows are supposed to renounce wealth and power. Choosing a life of virtue or of health can mean renouncing certain pleasures. Yet somehow, Christian moderates are leery of the idea of renunciation when it means cutting off toxic friends or walking away from white supremacist institutions. Maybe because this kind of renunciation might mean walking away from one's fellow Christians. We'd rather think of ourselves and our church as the good guys.

But thinking of ourselves as the good guys is one of the first things we need to renounce. And here is where Flannery O'Connor shines. Many of her stories highlight the difference between niceness and goodness, with respectable Christian protagonists having painful revelations about their own moral and spiritual poverty. The grandmother in "A Good Man Is Hard to Find," Mrs. Turpin in "Revelation," and the mother in "Everything That Rises Must Converge" are forced into positions of uncomfortable self-awareness. (Yes, these are all women, but I don't think O'Connor is being sexist. She's being accurate. Many women in conservative Christian culture, especially in small-town America, are like this. But anyone inclined to pride themselves on Christian superiority can probably "meet themselves coming and going" in O'Connor's fiction.)

Walker Percy, though less overtly, tells stories about letting go of self-absorption. This is an area where I can still take Percy seriously. He's uncomfortably on the nose when depicting the anxious, self-obsessed culture of the twentieth century, and I can only imagine what he'd have to say about the era of social media, with our fixation on followers and platforms and engagement, our selfies and reels, our filters, our Instagram faces.

But if you want to think about renunciation on a truly epic scale, Tolkien is the man. The entire saga of the One Ring is a story about the necessity of letting go of something that is enchanting, beautiful, compelling—and evil. The ultimate heroic task is not to fight or kill or defend but simply to let the thing go. Which turns out to be just about the hardest thing.

The two characters we see pass the test of the Ring in real time are Galadriel, the powerful elf-queen, and Samwise, the humble gardener. Both are heroes, equally, and both resist the temptation to possess the One Ring. And it turns out to be not just the Ring; heroism means being able to let things go and pass away. Sam keeps having to get rid of more and more of the small but treasured items he has carried with him, even his beloved cooking pans, and in the end, he only has the strength to carry Frodo up the mountain. Galadriel knows that with the passing of the Ring she will also have to accept the loss of Lorien and depart from Middle-earth—as

Sam, too, will do. As Aragorn says in *The Two Towers*, "One who cannot cast away a treasure at need is in fetters." He is commending Pippin for leaving his golden brooch on the trail as a sign to any trackers, but it's a moral for the larger story.

And this is crucial because of what happens to Frodo when he finally ascends the fiery mountain and finds that the One Ring has too great a hold on him. He cannot let it go. He cannot destroy it. This is a terrible moment, and one that Frodo will carry with him always, and not just because of the wound on his hand from Gollum attacking him and biting his finger off.

It wasn't until recently that I began to pay attention to a dimension of Frodo's trauma that I had not noticed in my younger days: he is not only scarred in body and mind, but he is ashamed. It's no accident that, throughout much of the last part of his journey, he and Gollum/Smeagol were so closely attuned to each other. Smeagol is reminded of his own long-ago days before he was warped by the Ring. But Gollum becomes Frodo's double or shadow-self, an image of who he will be if the Ring overwhelms him. So when the Ring finally takes possession, his own Gollum-side comes to the fore. But it is Gollum himself who inadvertently completes Frodo's mission. This is the shame that haunts Frodo: the specter of his own failure, the memory of his Gollum-self, maybe even the memory that it was Smeagol, in the end, who did the task he set out to do. It's easy to overlook this because Frodo is so heroic. He suffered unspeakably to save the Shire and all of Middle-earth. But for a brief moment, evil had complete possession of him. Yet, if he had not earlier, on multiple occasions, saved Smeagol, even trusted him, the quest truly would have failed.

This image of Frodo—heroic and revered, yet wounded, burdened with shame—is one I hope can be solace to other deconstructing readers who may be struggling with guilt over having been complicit in damaging movements and ideologies. Because Frodo is not defined by that moment on Mount Doom. He is defined by his courage along the way, his determination to do the right thing, and his mercy for Smeagol. And neither are we defined by the weakest, lowest moments in our past. But if ever we are tempted to hold onto oppressive principalities and powers, Tolkien's epic reminds us that it is never worth it. As Audre Lorde wrote in her powerful essay of the same name: "The master's tools will never dismantle the master's house." And the enchanted doorway in the garden wall can be a passage out, as well as a passage in.

Conclusion

Let's Do Better

We have a problem

One evening, around the time that I was wrapping up these final chapters, a group of Christians on social media were talking about how we need more thinkers like Chesterton. Since these were mostly progressive believers, I felt comfortable mentioning that, given how antisemitic, racist, and sexist Chesterton was, maybe we shouldn't be looking for the next Chesterton. Maybe we should be looking for Christian intellectual leaders among Black, womanist, feminist, and liberation theologians. The person who had initiated the conversation responded with mockery, then deleted my comment. I expect I came off as the quintessential shrill feminist, messing up the fun. Nearly all the people in the conversation were white men, so they probably found it easy to look past

Chesterton's bigotry, or write it off as "everyone was like that, back then."

Readers in progressive Christian literary spaces may feel that Christian bigotry is only a problem at more conservative institutions. They might point out that Christian literary culture has been expanding and diversifying for a while. We're now discussing the role of faith in the works of Toni Morrison, Louise Erdrich, Kirstin Valdez Quade, Maya Angelou, and Uwem Akpan. Perhaps they will note that in 2023, Georgetown University hosted a conference entitled the Global Aesthetics of the Catholic Imagination, which included a panel discussion on Catholic African and diaspora writers—or that the 2024 Catholic Imagination Conference at Notre Dame featured readings from Latina poets and a workshop on the Catholic imagination and disability.

But if we want our literary culture to reflect the gospel values of liberation, justice, and a preferential option for the marginalized, if we want our literary culture to reflect the diversity and universalism of the church, we still have a long way to go. We can't erase so easily the fact that our culture, literary and otherwise, was shaped by centuries of supremacy doctrines antithetical to the teachings of Jesus and to genuine virtue: antisemitism, patriarchy, sexism, classism, white supremacy, homophobia, colonialism, and disregard for those with chronic illness or disability.

We have this notion that at times when the world is in the thrall of evil, Christians are emboldened to take a stand for good. There are many examples of Christians who have done this: the Roman martyrs, Francis of Assisi, Teresa of Avila, Bartolome de las Casas, Frederick Douglass, Sojourner Truth, Dietrich Bonhoeffer, Dorothy Day, Martin Luther King, Jr., Oscar Romero. But do we see this heroic witness reflected in the Christian arts world? Not as much as we should. Our favorite writers were not on the forefront of justice movements. Some even resisted justice movements. It's not just that the modern Christian canon is very white and mostly male. It's that many of the writers we revere seem to have worked hard to keep it that way. Their work often perpetuates popular prejudices, unironically, and unquestioningly. And this legacy has shaped every one of our institutions, as well the stories we tell ourselves. True change will require deeper fixes than simply adding a few people from marginalized groups to a conference lineup.

One thing we will need to do is reevaluate how our dominant literary culture relates to its most beloved literary classics. We can start by admitting we have a problem—being honest about the fact that Christian culture, far from being a perennial beacon of truth and goodness, has often done serious harm, and that our literary culture was sometimes a part of this. This should not be news to us, especially to scholars and writers. For years, theologians, scholars, and activists from the demographics that were harmed have spoken out the real, unvarnished history of white patriarchal Christianity in the West. Especially in recent years, scholars have published important work on these topics, and I've included a short list of some of their books in the Recommended Reading section of this book.

Better conversations

In awakening to the reality of Christianity's history with justice and injustice, it becomes clear that we can no longer afford to deny or minimize harmful ideas in our intellectual and artistic traditions. Given the facts about the church in the Western world, it's impossible to pretend Chesterton wasn't antisemitic, or attempt to cast O'Connor as a heroic antiracist. Not because they "couldn't help it," or that theirs was "the default position at their time," but that bigotry was part of the package of their Christian inheritance. With that in mind, white and privileged readers should check themselves before trying to convince readers from marginalized groups that they are making things up or overreacting.

In a similar vein, it's not the job of those who are marginalized to adjust their tastes to meet the canon. If a canon of Christian classics holds to high standards of art making, ethics, and gospel teaching, it is the canon that has to be adjusted to accommodate facts, art, different understandings and perspectives, and morals. For the literary world to tell marginalized people that they are wrong to be offended, that they need to toughen up, or that they need to treat their own dehumanization as just a funny joke, is lazy and demeaning.

And even when we don't deliberately excuse harmful ideas, we still create a toxic environment in more subtle ways. Think about the message we communicate to communities of color, ethnic minorities, those in the disability community, and more, when we talk about books that dehumanize them, as the best that Christian literary culture has to offer. Or if we treat someone who was openly bigoted as a saint or moral hero. Or if we continue to ask questions like "where's our next Chesterton," instead of looking as Jesus continuously did, to the margins for the voices we've been missing, who not only have important things to say about the gospel, but who can infuse our literary culture with new, exciting, disrupting, and challenging perspectives.

Not all the books discussed in the previous chapters are equally problematic, of course. Sayers, Greene, and Tolkien are not toxic in the same way Chesterton is. But there's still the problem of including them as part of a body of literature that is white, colonialist, classist, heteronormative, and predominantly male—and treating that body of literature as the apex of Christian creativity.

Those of us who continue to enjoy these works might consider different contexts for reading, and remove them from that protective enclosure of white patriarchal Christianity. We can have such interesting conversations this way, too. Take Doreen Fowler or Nell Painter on Toni Morrison's critique of race in O'Connor, for instance. Or compare Lewis's depiction of gender in his *Space Trilogy* with Ursula K. LeGuin's in *The Left Hand of Darkness*.

Unfortunately, as my experience with the Chesterton fan highlighted, the dominant Christian literary culture doesn't always respond well to criticisms. Dominant cultures often have a bad habit of seeing even the gentlest critique—or other points of view—as an existential attack. There's a kind of entitlement that come from canon, a long history, and a politics of power in the religious literary world, a sense that one ought to be praised for doing even a bare minimum: "We included Toni Morrison, what more do you want?" Add Christianity's default posture of defensiveness, our Disney Princess theology, to that entitlement of power and position, and we have a toxic brew indeed. Maybe, actually, people dislike us because we are the oppressors?

Gioia claims that "most young writers no longer see their religion as a core identity—in spiritual or aesthetic terms. Their faith is something to be hidden or discarded in order to achieve success in an arts world that appears hostile to Christianity. In practical terms, who can blame them?"[1] But what he describes has not been my experience. Even when I was a conservative libertarian living in a super-progressive town, people were pretty tolerant of my ideological quirks. And I've never run into hostility toward my religion in secular-arts circles, and I'm far from the only religious writer in the literary groups I'm involved in. But there are a couple reasons why Gioia and others might perceive a hostility to Christianity in the secular literary world.

---

[1] Dana Gioia, "The Catholic Writer Today," *First Things*, December 2013.

First, because Christianity is now associated with bigotry, for multiple reasons that should be obvious. Earlier I asked: If my imagination was evangelized, what was it being evangelized into? Christianity, maybe, but Christianity without Christ. And that's what the world sees. The people in the arts world do not hate our beautiful ornate churches, our Latin chants, our rituals, our prayers, our holy water. But they have real reason to find homophobia, sexism, white supremacy, xenophobia, and a reverence for patriarchy harmful and problematic. And if they associate these things with Christianity, we have only ourselves to blame.

Second, because Christians have a bad habit of producing preachy, mediocre art. Gioia is writing specifically about Catholics, who have traditionally been fairly literary. But one outcome of the culture war is that Catholics have banded with white evangelicals, and created a subculture hostile to science, anti-intellectual, authoritarian, and reactionary, all antithetical to producing good art.

A way forward

So, no, we're not the victims in the story, nor are we the heroes, riding in like Gandalf on Shadowfax to save the day and evangelize the culture. We need to stop being so defensive. We need to stop patting ourselves on the back. And we definitely need to stop allowing our institutions to forgive abusers and elevate problematic characters.

As for expanding our horizons and honoring those voices that have continuously been marginalized by those declaring the canon, we can't do this in a tokenizing way. Simply adding a few non-white writers to a reading list or conference lineup does not make for a genuinely inclusive literary culture. Do we really understand just how much our literary culture benefits from and is enriched by a greater plurality of perspectives? Do we understand that the literary culture of Western Christendom was white-male-dominant for centuries because of systemic, hegemonic injustice, and that righting these wrongs takes work, not just a few checked boxes?

The white Western church has repeatedly communicated to marginalized demographics that they matter less than others. Celebrating books that dehumanize those demographics sends that message once again. We need to think objectively about our literary culture: How has it acted? How has it influenced the broader world? Has this culture been a force for good? Are we more just, more gospel-centered, more liberatory, more healing, than secular literary culture? How willing are we to take risks for the sake of the truth? Do we protect survivors and hold abusers accountable? Have we put our energy into justly distributing resources, or is influence consolidated in the hands of the privileged few? Are we willing to center and celebrate new writers from outside privileged demographics? Are we willing to decentralize our own power in order to do that? And are we willing to have the necessary hard conversations about our culture's complicity in harmful ideologies as well?

Instead of worrying about who is going to be the next Lewis, Greene, or O'Connor, perhaps we should be worried about what it means that we're still looking for the next Lewis, Greene, or O'Connor. Instead of congratulating ourselves on our possession of some unique treasure trove of truth and beauty to offer a stricken world, maybe we should put more work into interrogating our own complicity in a problematic heritage. Repentance and soul-searching might be good for us, and good for our stories, too. There's a lot to be written about penitence and atonement, about healing and starting over.

Then maybe our literary culture can start to become what we imagine it to be.

Recommended Reading

Books on Christianity's Complicity in Ideologies of Hate

Disciples of White Jesus by Angela Denker (Minneapolis: Broadleaf Books, 2025).

The Catholic Church and the Struggle for Racial Justice by Matt Kappadakunnel (Mahwah, NJ: Paulist Press, 2024).

In the Shadow of Freedom by Alessandra Harris (Maryknoll, NY: Orbis Books, 2024).

The Hidden Roots of White Supremacy and the Path to a Shared American Future by Robert P. Jones (New York: Simon and Schuster, 2023).

All Oppression Shall Cease by Christopher Kellerman, SJ (Maryknoll, NY: Orbis Books, 2022).

The Making of Biblical Womanhood: How the Subjugation of Women Became Gospel Truth by Beth Allison Barr (Grand Rapids, MI: Brazos Press, 2021).

Christianity Corrupted: The Scandal of White Supremacy by Jermaine Marshall (Maryknoll, NY: Orbis Books, 2021).

Women: Icons of Christ by Phyllis Zagano (Mahwah, NJ: Paulist Press, 2020).

The Christian Imagination: Theology and the Origins of Race by Willie James Jennings (New Haven, CT: Yale University Press, 2011).

The Cross and the Lynching Tree by James H. Cone (Maryknoll, NY: Orbis Books, 2011).

Holy Hatred: Christianity, Antisemitism, and the Holocaust by Robert Michael (London: Palgrave Macmillan, 2006).

Christian Antisemitism: A History of Hate by William Nicholls (Lanham, MD: Jason Aronson, 1995).

Sexism and God Talk: Toward a Feminist Theology by Rosemary Radford Ruether (Boston: Beacon Press, 1993).

Bibliography

Adichie, Chimamanda Ngozi. "The Danger of a Single Story." TED Talks.

Bosco, Mark, SJ. "Flannery O'Connor: A Walking Contradiction on Race." *America*, July 17, 2020.

Burton, Poppy. "Everything Wrong with the 'Tortured Artist' Trope." *Far Out*, July 30, 2023.

Caplan-Bricker, Nora. "An Overlooked Novel from 1935, by the Godmother of Feminist Detective Fiction." *The New Yorker*, November 13, 2019.

Chesterton, G. K. *The Annotated Innocence of Father Brown.* Edited by Martin Gardner. Mineola, NY: Dover Publications, 1998.

———. *Divorce versus Democracy.* Project Gutenberg. June 24, 2020.

———. *Father Brown and the Church of Rome.* Edited by John Peterson. San Francisco: Ignatius Press, 1996.

Denker, Angela. *Disciples of White Jesus: The Radicalization of American Boyhood.* Minneapolis: Broadleaf Books, 2025.

Elie, Paul. "How Racist Was Flannery O'Connor?" *The New Yorker*, June 15, 2020.

Eliot, T. S. *The Complete Poems and Plays*. New York: Harcourt Brace and Company, 1967.

———. "Tradition and the Individual Talent." *The Sacred Wood and Major Early Essays*. Dover Publications, 1997.

Flieger, Verlyn. "The Arch and the Keystone." *Mythlore: A Journal of J. R. R. Tolkien, C. S. Lewis, Charles Williams, and Mythopoeic Literature* 38, no. 1, art. 3 (October 2019).

Gioia, Dana. "The Catholic Writer Today." *First Things*, December 2013.

Gopnik, Adam. "The Next Thing." *The New Yorker*, January 19, 2015.

Grabowski, Joe. "A Lesson in Localism." *Gilbert: The Magazine of the Society of G. K. Chesterton* 27, no. 6 (July/August 2024).

Granger, Ben. "The Literary and Political Catholicism of Graham Greene and Evelyn Waugh." *Spike Magazine*, May 19, 2008.

Greene, Graham. *Brighton Rock*. New York: Bantam Books, 1968.

Hackett, Erna Kim. "Why I Stopped Talking about Racial Reconciliation and Started Talking about White Supremacy." *Inheritance*, March 25, 2020.

Hagi, Sarah. "Cancel Culture Is Not Real—At Least Not in the Way People Think." *Time,* November 21, 2019.

Hall, Cassidy. "A Sideways Glance." *US Catholic* 89, no. 10 (October 2024).

Hart, David Bentley. "A Person You Flee at Parties." *First Things,* May 6, 2011.

Jemison, Elizabeth L. "Proslavery Christianity after the Emancipation." *Tennessee Historical Quarterly* 72, no. 4 (Winter 2013).

Kohlhaas, Jacob. "When Did the Church Condemn Slavery?" *US Catholic,* November 6, 2023.

Levantovskaya, Maggie. "On Flannery O'Connor's Chronic Illness . . . and Chronic Racism." *Literary Hub*, August 6, 2020.

Lewis, C. S. *Out of the Silent Planet.* New York: Scribner, 1938.

———. *That Hideous Strength.* New York: Scribner, 1945.

Oakes, Kaya. *Not So Sorry: Abusers, False Apologies, and the Limits of Forgiveness.* Minneapolis: Broadleaf Books, 2024.

O'Donnell, Angela Alaimo. "The 'Canceling' of Flannery O'Connor?" *Commonweal,* August 3, 2020.

Oliverio, Lisa. "Disability in Flannery O'Connor's Fiction." *Interdisciplinary Journal of the Dedicated Semester* 2 (2011).

Percy, Walker. *Love in the Ruins.* New York: Farrar, Straus and Giroux, 1971.

———. "Stoicism in the South." *Commonweal*, July 6, 1956.

Pew Research Center. "Modeling the Future of Religion in America," September 13, 2022.

Pratt, Tia Noelle. "'I Bring Myself, My Black Self.'" *Commonweal*, November 3, 2020,

Ross, Frederick A. *Slavery Ordained of God*. Philadelphia, 1857; Project Gutenberg.

Royal, Robert. "The (Mis)guided Dream of Graham Greene." *First Things*, November 1999.

Sayers, Dorothy. *Gaudy Night*. New York: HarperPaperbacks, 1995.

Schwartz, Amy E. "The Curious Case of Dorothy L. Sayers and the Jew Who Wasn't There." *Moment*, July-August 2016.

Tolkien, J. R. R. *The Letters of J. R. R. Tolkien*. Edited by Humphrey Carpenter. Boston: Mariner Books, 2000.

———. *The Lord of the Rings*, Boston: Houghton Mifflin Company, 2004.

Tolkien, Simon. "Tolkien's Grandson on How WW1 Inspired *The Lord of the Rings*." BBC, January 3, 2017.

Vorachek, Laura. "His Appearance Is against Him": Race and Criminality in Dorothy L. Sayers's *Unnatural Death*." *Clues: A Journal of Detection* 37, no. 2 (Fall 2019).

Waugh, Evelyn. *Brideshead Revisited*. New York: Little, Brown, and Company, 1999.

Wilson, Jessica Hooten. "How Flannery O'Connor Fought Racism." *First Things,* June 24, 2020.

Wiman, Christian. *Zero at the Bone: Fifty Entries against Despair.* New York: Farrar, Straus, and Giroux, 2023.

Acknowledgments

My editor, Lil Copan. With gratitude for excellent guidance.

Jessica Mesman, for putting ideas in my head, and encouraging me to pitch this book. There's no muse like a good art friend.

My brother, Jonathan Bratten, military historian, for directing me to accurate information about the Civil War, Reconstruction, and the American South, and for helping me hash out some of the details on Chesterton, Lewis, and Tolkien.

My sister, Joanna Bratten, English literature scholar and expert on Waugh and Greene, for directing me to scholarship on those two, answering my prurient questions about their shenanigans, and speculating with me about which one of them would be more fun to drink with (Greene, all the way).

John Farrell, for bouncing ideas around, offering encouragement, and supporting my rants.

The Sick Pilgrim arts community, for reading, writing, and deconstructing with me through the years.

Sean Dailey, for conversations about Tolkien and resources on Tolkien's white supremacist fans.

And thanks to Brendan, Dominic, Avila, and Gideon, who put up with my many evening disappearances to my study. Now that this is wrapped up maybe I can join in game night again.